REPUTATIONS

LINCOLN

Andrew Lee

B.T. BATSFORD LTD, LONDON

Typeset by Tek-Art Ltd, Kent
and printed in Great Britain by
The Bath Press
Bath
for the publishers
B.T. Batsford Ltd
4 Fitzhardinge Street
London W1H 0AH

ISBN 0 7134 5662 0

Acknowledgments

The Author and Publishers would like to thank the
following for permission to reproduce illustrations: BBC
Hulton Picture Library for the frontispiece and pages 5,
7, 8a, 9, 14, 15, 16, 17, 20, 21, 24, 25, 32, 40, 48, 50a, 53,
57, 58 and 60; Margaret Killingray for page 27; The
Mandel Archive for pages 23b, 44 and 55; The Mansell
Collection for pages 6, 8b, 13, 23a, 35, 43, 46a, 46b, 47,
50b, 51a, 51b and 54. The maps on pages 26 and 49 were
drawn by Robert Brien.

Frontispiece   *Image of Lincoln from a campaign poster for
the 1860 Presidential election.*

Cover Illustrations

(clockwise from top left): *The Lincoln Memorial, Washington
D.C.* (courtesy BBC Hulton Picture Library); *Lincoln
and his son Tad* (courtesy The Mansell Collection);
Lincoln the Lawyer: the first portrait of Lincoln (courtesy
BBC Hulton Picture Library); *Long Abraham* (courtesy
The Mandel Archive); and *The Overdue Bill* (courtesy
BBC Hulton Picture Library).

Contents

Time Chart

1809	Birth of Abraham Lincoln in Kentucky.
1816	Lincoln family move to Indiana.
1818	Death of Nancy Lincoln, Abraham's natural mother.
1819	Thomas Lincoln marries Sarah Johnston.
1820	The Missouri Compromise.
1830	Lincoln family move to Illinois.
1834	Abraham Lincoln elected to Illinois State Legislature.
1836	Abraham Lincoln admitted to the Illinois Bar.
1837	Abraham Lincoln moves to Springfield, the new state capital of Illinois.
1842	Abraham Lincoln marries Mary Todd.
1843	Birth of Robert Todd Lincoln.
1845	Annexation of Texas.
1846	War with Mexico.
	Abraham Lincoln elected to the Congress of the United States as Representative for Illinois.
	Birth of Edward Baker Lincoln.
1849	Abraham Lincoln returns to his law practice in Springfield.
1850	Death of Edward Lincoln.
	The Compromise of 1850.
	Birth of William Wallace Lincoln.
1851	Death of Thomas Lincoln, Abraham's father.
1853	Birth of Thomas Lincoln (junior).
1854	The Kansas-Nebraska Act.
	Abraham Lincoln elected to the Illinois State Legislature.
1856	Abraham Lincoln joins the new Republican Party.
1858	Abraham Lincoln stands as candidate for the Senate of the United States.
	The Lincoln-Douglas Debates.
1860	Abraham Lincoln elected President of the United States.
1861	4 March: Lincoln inaugurated as President. 14 April: fall of Fort Sumter.
1862	Death of William Lincoln.
	22 September Proclamation of Emancipation.
1865	9 April: Surrender of Lee.
	14 April: Assassination of Lincoln.

The Reputation

'Larger than Life'

Abraham Lincoln, sixteenth President of the United States of America, was shot by an assassin on 14 April 1865, and died the next morning. His body then lay in state at the White House, before making its last earthly journey, through Baltimore, Harrisburg, Philadelphia, New York, Albany, Buffalo, Cleveland, Columbus, Indianapolis and Chicago. During almost the entire railroad journey, and at various stops for the coffin to lie in state, crowds of mourners watched with bowed heads. In the major cities there were great demonstrations and processions. Often prominent, according to contemporary sources, were soldiers from the recently victorious Union army, and negroes; in New York 200 black men carried a banner which read, 'Abraham Lincoln – Our Emancipator'. Eventually, on 4 May, Lincoln was buried at Oakland Cemetry in his home town of Springfield, Illinois, alongside the body of his young son Willie.

Lincoln's assassination inevitably turned him in to a martyr and a hero:

. . . the overwhelming aspect of his reputation is that he was assassinated, and so he was canonized, because a halo descends on all the murdered Presidents, and on Lincoln most of all.

Alistair Cooke's America, BBC Publications 1973.

Alistair Cooke is a famous American journalist and commentator, born in England in 1908.

Abraham Lincoln, complete with saintly aura.

Very raised picture the saintly aura suggest Lincoln was more then a leader he was a saviour of country and people

Booth looks as if he intends to succeed as he shoots Abraham Lincoln. Booth and Mrs Lincoln are very accurately drawn. The others in the box are Major Henry R. Rathbone and his fiancée, Clara Harris. The play was an English comedy Our American Cousin.

See p. 52.

The process started straight away. Almost before his body was cold, people were seeking souvenirs: a piece of blood-stained bedlinen, a lock of hair. Then the eulogies appeared, such as that by Ralph Waldo Emerson. Before long, Lincoln's legal partner, William Herndon, was lecturing and writing misleadingly about the man he had known; and Lincoln's friends and acquaintances from Illinois were dusting off their reminiscences about the frontier lawyer who made it to the White House. The 'official' biography was soon written by Lincoln's wartime secretaries, Nicolay and Hay, portraying him as the tough, salt-of-the-earth Westerner but elevating him almost to the status of a demigod.

Since then the mythology has continued to grow. There are societies dedicated to his memory, and the study of Lincoln has become almost an academic industry (the historical literature is *vast*). His name has been used, either honestly or corruptly, to sanctify many different political causes in the United States. The places associated with his life have been turned into shrines. Though he was undoubtedly a great man, he has become larger than life – he has been carved into the side of a mountain at Mount Rushmore, and his seated, angular figure looks out from a marble temple at Washington. As the nineteenth-century historian Ida Tarbell wrote:

From the day of his death until now, the world has gone on rearing monuments to Abraham Lincoln.
Ida Tarbell, *The Life of Abraham Lincoln*, Vol. II, Doubleday Page & Co., 1895.

The main outlines of the heroic image are clear. Lincoln was born and grew up on the frontier, which in those days had only just reached the Mississippi. He was bold, strong, a voracious reader and had turned his hand to most of the occupations of a pioneer – he had guided a plough, split fence rails, piloted a flat boat and fought Indians. He had then turned himself in to a surveyor and later a successful frontier lawyer, defending the right, the innocent and the exploited. Entering the arena of national politics in order to fight the extension of slavery, the integrity, common sense and down-to-earth wisdom of 'Honest Abe' swept him into the White House at a crucial stage in American history. He fought the Southerners who wanted to leave the Union over the issue of slavery (and were in the wrong), and in the Civil War he kept the United States together and freed the slaves (all of which was right).

SURRAT. BOOTH. HAROLD.

War Department, Washington, April 20, 1865,

$100,000 REWARD!

THE MURDERER

Of our late beloved President, Abraham Lincoln,

IS STILL AT LARGE.

$50,000 REWARD

Will be paid by this Department for his apprehension, in addition to any reward offered by Municipal Authorities or State Executives.

$25,000 REWARD

Will be paid for the apprehension of JOHN H. SURRATT, one of Booth's Accomplices.

$25,000 REWARD

Will be paid for the apprehension of David C. Harold, another of Booth's accomplices.

LIBERAL REWARDS will be paid for any information that shall conduce to the arrest of either of the above-named criminals, or their accomplices.

All persons harboring or secreting the said persons, or either of them, or aiding or assisting their concealment or escape, will be treated as accomplices in the murder of the President and the attempted assassination of the Secretary of State, and shall be subject to trial before a Military Commission and the punishment of DEATH.

Let the stain of innocent blood be removed from the land by the arrest and punishment of the murderers.

All good citizens are exhorted to aid public justice on this occasion. Every man should consider his own conscience charged with this solemn duty, and rest neither night nor day until it be accomplished.

EDWIN M. STANTON, Secretary of War.

DESCRIPTIONS.—BOOTH is Five Feet 7 or 8 inches high, slender build, high forehead, black hair, black eyes, and wears a heavy black moustache.

JOHN H. SURRAT is about 5 feet, 9 inches. Hair rather thin and dark; eyes rather light; no beard. Would weigh 145 or 150 pounds. Complexion rather pale and clear, with color in his cheeks. Wore light clothes of fine quality. Shoulders square; cheek bones rather prominent; chin narrow; ears projecting at the top; forehead rather low and square, but broad. Parts his hair on the right side; neck rather long. His lips are firmly set. A slim man.

DAVID C. HAROLD is five feet six inches high, hair dark, eyes dark, eyebrows rather heavy, full face, nose short, hand short and fleshy, feet small, instep high, round bodied, naturally quick and active, slightly closes his eyes when looking at a person.

NOTICE.—In addition to the above, State and other authorities have offered rewards amounting to almost one hundred thousand dollars, making an aggregate of about TWO HUNDRED THOUSAND DOLLARS.

Booth was hunted down to a barn in Virginia and shot by federal troops. Four of Booth's associates were captured and hanged.

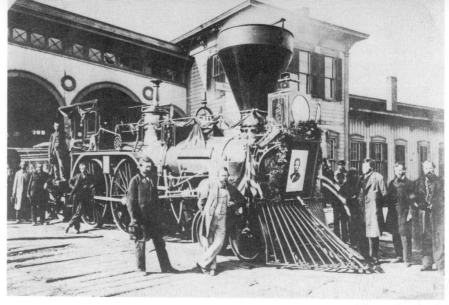

The locomotive 'Nashville', suitably decorated to haul Lincoln's funeral train. Photographic exposure times were long, which may be why some of the railroad officials are leaning against the engine.

Then there are the details of the heroic image, too many to deal with here, but some stand out: the way he had ignored party and personal considerations in order to win the Civil War, his sincerity, his humility, his steadfastness and consistency, his understanding of people.

And if all that is not enough, there is the wealth of anecdote and hearsay about him – about his marriage, his children, his famous habit of telling jokes and stories to illustrate an important point, even in Cabinet meetings. It seems that everybody who knew him had at least one story to tell.

Perhaps the most powerful image of Lincoln is his physical appearance, for he can be seen in a remarkable series of photographic portraits which reveal the physical effects of age and the strain of leadership. He was a tall man, well over six foot (1.84 metres), with a gaunt frame, long arms and legs and large feet and hands. He had a full head of black, rather untidy hair, a high forehead, prominent nose and deep, knowing eyes, which in the photographs gaze mournfully into the distance (possibly a consequence of the formal poses and long exposure times required in the early days of photography). Accounts also tell of his shambling gait and ill-fitting clothes, especially of the way in which his thin and rather long neck protruded from over-size collars. For all its peculiarity, his physical appearance has become part of the legend as well.

However, the modern-day common sense of Alistair Cooke is worth some attention:

It is difficult, and in some quarters thought to be almost tasteless to talk sense about Lincoln. But we must try. For the holy image and the living man were very

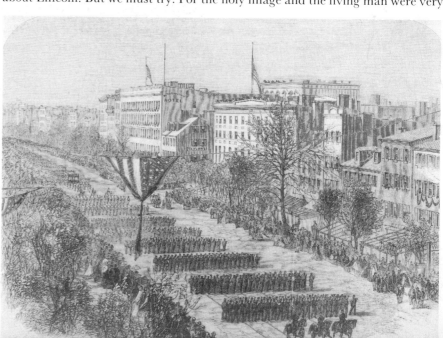

Lincoln's funeral procession through Washington.

far apart, and keeping them so does no service either to Lincoln or to the art of government.
Alistair Cooke's America.

The fact is that Lincoln was human, and in his lifetime he made mistakes, suffered from shortcomings, experienced self-doubt and failure, and was hated as much as he was loved. When he was alive his name was frequently mentioned not in tones of reverence, but of spiteful derision. Hostile journalists called him, 'a slang-whanging stump speaker', 'a half-witted usurper', or quite simply, 'the Baboon'. A *Punch* cartoon by Tenniel, at the time of the *Trent* incident, portrayed Lincoln as a frightened racoon, taking refuge up a tree to escape the anger of John Bull. His humility was regarded as hypocrisy by his opponents; his refusal to campaign in the Presidential elections of 1860 and 1864 was sneered at by critics, who said (in an age when classical references were more understood than they are now) that he was pretending to be like Cincinnatus tending his plough. A neighbour in Springfield had a more direct way of summing him up, describing him as just plain crafty and dishonest (a view which most Southerners would have shared). Lincoln's caution and sagacity, 'gave rise to the whisper of, "cunning as a fox".'

Most significant is the point that many history books tend to assume that Lincoln was right about slavery and the permanence of the Federal Union, but many Americans at the time (perhaps even a majority) thought he was wrong. Certainly the opponents of Lincoln had as many good arguments as he did by the standards of the day.

Nevertheless, there were aspects of Lincoln that *did* make him great. His dignity, tolerance, avoidance of doctrinaire solutions and sound politcal judgment about when to act and when to forbear, all turned him in to a successful war leader in a democracy. His failures and weaknesses do not take anything away. Instead, they enhance his greatness and show that like most of us he was a mixture of parts: ambitious but doubtful of his own worth, forceful but thoughtful and reflective, gifted with wit and dry humour but given to bouts of depression. Would he have achieved as much if he had been arrogant, self-assured, insensitive and dogmatic?

In 1861 a Union (Northern) warship stopped the British ship *Trent* and seized two Confederate (Southern) commissioners bound for Britain. British reaction forced the North to 'cheerfully liberate' the commissioners.

In the early days of the Roman Republic peasant farmer Cincinnatus, who was without personal ambition, assumed the Dictatorship and saved Rome from its enemies; he then returned to agricultural life.

Carl Sandburg, an American historian who has written widely on Lincoln, in *Prairie Years*, Vol. II.

Lincoln enthroned on symbols of unity.
The Lincoln Memorial, Washington D.C.

The Background

A Nation in the Making

The Constitution

In May 1787, 55 delegates from the original 13 states of the USA met in Philadelphia to write a new Constitution for their recently created country. These men were the 'Founding Fathers', and included individuals of undoubted greatness: Franklin, Washington, Madison and Hamilton. Two great names were missing, for Jefferson and John Adams were acting as envoys in Europe.

The Founding Fathers were attempting to make a nation. This was a novel, daring but necessary experiment in a world which at that time was full of countries ruled by hereditary monarchs, whose laws and powers had evolved through tradition and custom. The United States had itself come in to being only in 1776, when the 13 British colonies in North America made their Declaration of Independence. Bitter fighting had followed until 1783, when the British recognized that they could not subjugate the colonies at an acceptable price and signed the Treaty of Paris, granting independence to the 13 States. At that time the United States had a loose form of Constitution known as the Articles of Confederation. But the troubled early years of the young republic showed that the Articles were not really good enough. A new set of rules would have to be written to prevent the United States from falling apart (as most Europeans at the time thought it would). Thus it was that the 55 delegates made the difficult journey to the Pennsylvania State House, now called Independence Hall, in Philadelphia.

They had a very complicated job, and it is with the Constitution that they wrote that we need to start if we are going to understand the career of Abraham Lincoln. They decided that the United States should be ruled by an elected President and that the laws of the United States should be made and the taxes levied by an elected Congress. Congress would contain two 'houses', the upper house being the Senate and the lower house being the House of Representatives. This much was necessary to provide strong national government to hold the United States together. However, as much power as possible was retained for the individual states of the United States. This was because the new nation had been born out of the fear of oppressive British rule. They were not about to throw away the liberty that they had so recently won by handing all power over to the new government. Thus the individual states retained control over many matters including police, education, transport, marriage laws, voting rights, citizenship and the existence of slavery. The laws and policies of each individual state would be decided upon by a state governor and an elected state legislature.

Another important part of the new Constitution was the Supreme Court. The Supreme Court is the highest court in the United States. It is made up of nine judges appointed by the President. Its job is to interpret the

The American War of Independence. The British King George III attempted to suppress the 13 colonies, which were led by George Washington.

Constitution and laws of the United States. In practice, this means that the Supreme Court decides whether or not the actions of the President, states, Congress or anybody else, are constitutional.

However, the new Constitution still left many issues unclear. For the purposes of our story the two most important unresolved issues were states' rights and slavery.

States' rights

Washington: President of the USA 1789-97.

Hamilton: Secretary of the Treasury under Washington's Presidency.

Jefferson: Secretary of State (Foreign Minister) 1790-93 and Vice-President 1797-1801.

The Founding Fathers disagreed about the precise balance of power between the federal government (the President and Congress in Washington D.C.) and the governments of the individual states. 'Federalists' such as Washington and Hamilton believed in a broad interpretation of the Constitution, which gave the federal government wide powers to pass measures for the general good of the nation. But 'Republicans' such as Jefferson wanted the balance of power to favour the individual states, and believed that the actions of the federal government should be hemmed in by a strict interpretation of the new Constitution. Jefferson believed that the federal government should only do precisely that which the Constitution said it could do.

Which view of states' rights, the Federalist or the Republican, was correct? On the one hand, Article I, Section 8 of the Constitution says:

Imposts and excises: indirect taxes levied on goods within a country.

The Congress shall have power to lay and collect taxes, Duties, Imposts and Excises, to pay the Debts and provide for the common Defence and General Welfare of the United States . . .

This could be broadly interpreted by the Federalists as supporting their position. But on the other hand Amendment X of the Constitution, passed in 1789, says:

The powers not delegated to the United States by the Constitution; nor prohibited by it to the States, are reserved to the States respectively, or to the people.

This appears to mean that unless the Constitution specifically gives a particular power or responsibility to the federal government, then that power or responsibility belongs to the individual states. Clearly this supports a Republican viewpoint.

The Constitution, then, does not give a cut-and-dried answer to the question of states' rights, and a significant part of United States' history up to the time of the Civil War was concerned with working out where in practice federal power ended and state power began.

During the Presidency of George Washington (1789 to 1797) the brilliant young Secretary of the Treasury, Alexander Hamilton, implemented an economic policy under which the federal government assumed significant powers. Taxes and tariffs were introduced, but the measure which really raised the issue of states' rights for the first time was the creation of the Bank of the United States. Federalists argued that the creation of a national bank would aid economic growth and stabilize national finances. However, Madison and Jefferson argued that the whole Federalist economic programme was bestowing too much power on the federal government. In particular, they said that Congress had no power under the Constitution to charter a bank which could operate throughout the Union; the power to authorize a bank within a state belonged to the state itself. Hamilton replied that the government *was* empowered by the Constitution to do whatever was 'necessary and proper' for the general benefit of the nation.

As it turned out, Hamilton's economic policies went forward and were generally very successful. But battle had been joined over a major aspect of the Constitution. Meanwhile, there had been another local incident which was a pointer to things to come. This was the Whiskey Rebellion which occurred in the more remote parts of Pennsylvania. In the mountains, farmers turned their grain surpluses into whiskey, which could be exchanged almost like currency. However, one of Hamilton's policies was to put an excise on whiskey in order to help pay off the debts incurred during the War of Independence. The 'moonshiners' objected to this tax on their activities and felt that it was highly unfair that they should be paying off other people's debts in this way. President Washington met this resistance by marching 15,000 militiamen to western Pennsylvania, at which the revolt collapsed. However, this episode showed that in addition to the issue of states' rights, there were also going to be problems where local *sectional* interests conflicted with those of national policy.

During the Presidency of the Federalist John Adams (1797 to 1801) the argument over states' rights took another step forward. With the French Revolutionary Wars going on in Europe, Adams was very sensitive to Republican criticism and to the activities of foreign agents and new immigrants who might have Republican sympathies. Consequently, Adams passed the Alien and Sedition Laws, which restrained the activities of enemy aliens in time of war, tightened up on the naturalization of new arrivals in America, and cracked down on the expression of criticism aimed at the government. The Republicans believed these acts to be unconstitutional, but could get no support from the Supreme Court. Consequently, Madison and Jefferson secured the passage of resolutions in the state legislatures of Virginia and Kentucky. These claimed that individual states had the right to nullify federal legislation which they believed to be unconstitutional. If this doctrine of nullification held good it would be an important addition to the rights of the states. However, for the time being the issue subsided with the election of Jefferson as President. The Alien and Sedition Laws lapsed following Jefferson's inauguration in 1801.

The problem of states' rights continued to intrude into American national life. For example, the Bank controversy raised its head again in 1819 when the state of Maryland claimed that the Bank of the United States had no right to issue bank notes within Maryland's boundaries. On this occasion the federal government won, for Chief Justice Marshall of the Supreme Court, the most distinguished of early American jurists, found in favour of the Bank.

By the late 1820s the Federalist Party had died away. But the Republicans had split into two factions: the National Republicans led by John Quincy Adams, and the Democratic Republicans led by Andrew Jackson. The National Republicans, later to be known as Whigs, believed in spending federal money on improvements such as roads and canals. They also believed in protective tariffs on manufactured goods and the continued existence of a federally chartered Bank. The Democratic Republicans, or just plain Democrats, had a less clearly defined programme but tended to support states' rights and were hostile to the Bank of the United States. Democratic Republicanism was really about the rugged pioneer individualism of the spreading frontier areas beyond the Appalachians, although Jackson also received support from working men in most parts of the United States.

Jackson, a tough old Indian fighter who had also defeated the British at New Orleans during the short-lived war of 1812-1814, became President in 1829. His track record would lead one to suppose that he should have been

The French Revolution of 1789-99 abolished absolute monarchy and established a republic.

Nullify: to make the legislation invalid.

Henry Clay of Kentucky, the 'Great Compromiser'.

a supporter of states' rights, but in fact he became involved in a very important attempt to impose federal authority. In order to win the election of 1828 Jackson and his rather devious political adviser Martin van Buren had accidentally saddled the United States with an exceptionally high tariff on imports. South Carolina, led by the fiery John C. Calhoun, bitterly objected to the tariff. Like all of the Southern states, South Carolina had to buy the majority of its manufactured goods either from the Northern industrial states or from Europe. They believed, therefore, that the tariff on imports merely allowed the Northern manufacturers to charge higher prices for their own products, thereby profiteering at the expense of the Southerners. Calhoun claimed that the tariff was unconstitutional on the grounds that it benefited some states but injured others. He went on to claim that South Carolina had the right to nullify the 'Tariff of Abominations'. South Carolina began to resist the federal excise officers and Jackson prepared to send federal troops to enforce the tariff, even threatening to have Calhoun shot. The crisis ended in a compromise arranged by Henry Clay, a Whig known as the 'Great Compromiser', who was the political hero of Abraham Lincoln.

However, the issue of states' rights was still not settled. Could a state nullify legislation that it disliked, or which harmed its sectional interests? The answer was not clear. And underneath this question there lurked an even more dangerous one: what if a state disliked federal legislation so much that it wanted to withdraw from the Union? Had a state the right to secede? This was not just an academic question. By the middle of the century there *was* an issue over which the southern states would at least talk about secession: slavery.

Secede: to withdraw from the Union.

The slavery issue

Negro slavery existed in most of the colonies before 1776. By the end of the eighteenth century most of the more northerly states had abolished slavery, but in the Southern states it was retained. Slavery was not really economically worthwhile in the North, where commerce, manufacturing, hay, dairy and grain farming were best carried out using wage labour. But in the South plantation crops such as cotton, rice and sugar required permanent supplies of cheap labour; negro slavery was used to provide this. In fact, it looked as if slavery would die out in the South also, for the coastal

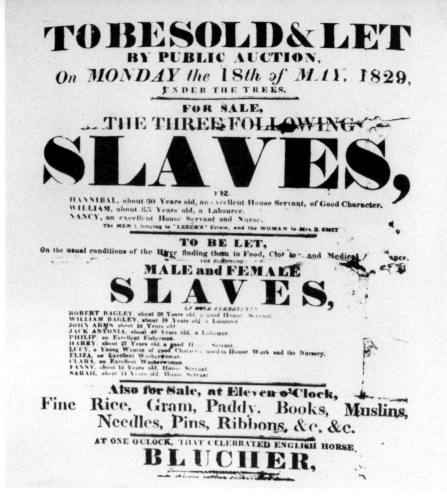

Human beings for sale.

cotton growing areas of the Carolinas were becoming exhausted and the mechanized cotton textile industry of Britain obtained most of its raw materials from elsewhere. However, in 1793 Eli Whitney invented the cotton gin. This machine removed the seeds from previously unsuitable 'short staple' cotton which could be successfully grown inland. 'Uplands' cotton rapidly became an industrial crop and guaranteed that slavery would continue in the South.

Nowadays we should utterly condemn slavery, but what did the Founding Fathers have to say about it in the Constitution? The truth is that they said very little about it; indeed they did not mention it by name. There were enough problems involved in agreeing the Constitution without adding one more to the list. Certainly there were men who would have wished to abolish slavery, but in practice the Constitution tacitly accepted its existence. Article I says:

The number of representatives sent to the lower house of Congress is proportional to the population of the state. For the purposes of counting the population the Constitution originally said by implication that a slave counted as three-fifths of a free man (the 'federal ratio').

Representatives and direct Taxes shall be apportioned among the several States which may be included within this Union, according to their respective Numbers, which shall be determined by adding to the whole Number of free Persons, including those bound to service for a Term of Years, and excluding Indians not taxed, three fifths of all other Persons.

Article IV says:

This implied, firstly, that it was up to each state to make its own laws about slavery, and, secondly, that runaway slaves had to be returned if they escaped to 'free states'.

No Person held to Service or Labour in one State, under the laws thereof, escaping into another, shall, in consequence of any Law or Regulation therein, be discharged from any such Service or Labour, but shall be delivered up on claim of the Party to whom such Service or Labour may be due.

However, it is an open question as to what the founding Fathers thought should happen to slavery in the future. Whether or not they expected the eventual abolition of slavery was debated by Lincoln and Douglas in the 1850s (see p. 30), but it is clear that the Founding Fathers were wary of allowing the *extension* of slavery. Under the North West Territorial Ordinance of 1787 slavery was excluded from the area south of the Great Lakes which had been acquired from Britain in the Treaty of Paris. In 1808 the transatlantic slave trade was outlawed by Act of Congress.

But the existence of slavery could not be ignored, because the boundaries of the United States were expanding westwards. In 1803, Jefferson made the Louisiana Purchase from France, and acquired a huge tract of land between the Mississippi and the Rocky Mountains. Step by step this area was settled by immigrants and Easterners. By 1819 a part of the Louisiana Purchase called the Missouri Territory had sufficient settlers to apply for statehood and found itself the focus of an exceedingly heated slavery debate. Should Missouri be admitted to the Union as a slave or a non-slave state?

The problem was that by this time there were 11 slave states in the Union and 11 non-slave states. Each section feared that if the other achieved a majority in the Senate by the admission of new states then the political balance in the Union would be permanently tilted one way or the other.

The solution was Henry Clay's Missouri Compromise of 1820. Missouri entered the Union as a slave state but at the same time Maine (in the North) was admitted as a free state. In future, states would 'pair up' in this way in order to join the Union. All territories within the Louisiana Purchase north of 36°30′ (Missouri's southern boundary) would not be allowed to adopt slavery.

For a decade and a half the Missouri Compromise preserved the peace, but during the Presidency of James Knox Polk the 'manifest destiny' of the United States to stretch from the Atlantic to the Pacific was fulfilled. The question arose: what should be the future of slavery in the colossal regions acquired by the annexation of Texas (1845), the Mexican War (1846-8) and the Oregon Treaty (1846)?

Throughout the eighteenth century French settlers had been colonizing Louisiana and the area between the Great Lakes.

As a result of war with Mexico the United States gained a vast area in the South-West, stretching south from Utah to Mexico and across to California. The Oregon Treaty was concluded with Britain and established the north-western boundary between between the United States and Canada.

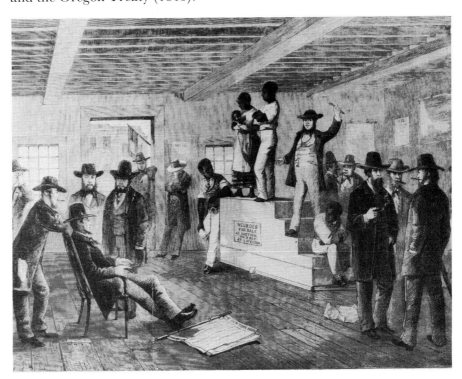

A slave auction in Virginia, 1861. Nobody seems to be buying.

A fugitive slave is captured. This sort of incident, together with popular novels such as Uncle Tom's Cabin *by Harriet Beecher Stowe, reinforced Northern dislike of slavery.*

Abolitionists: those who wanted the complete abolition of slavery.

Texas already had slavery, dating from the time when it had been Mexican territory. Would the other vast area gained from Mexico, known broadly as California, also fall into the hands of the slavers? David Wilmot, a Democrat from Pennsylvania, thought that it should not. With the backing of northern Whigs, Abraham Lincoln among them, he proposed the 'proviso' that 'neither slavery not involuntary servitude shall ever exist in any part of said territory'.

The slavery and states' rights issues had intersected. Did the federal government have the power to ban slavery in the territories? Faced by fierce Southern opposition, the Wilmot Proviso continued to be debated until 1849, when the whole situation took a fresh turn. The population of the Pacific South-West had rocketed upwards following the discovery of gold. In 1849 and 1850 respectively, California and New Mexico applied to enter the Union. Their proposed constitutions expressly forbade slavery. A renewed crisis followed in which both slavers and abolitionists started to gather their forces. By the time that the 73-year-old Henry Clay put together his last great compromise, virtually all the arguments which in 1860 led to civil war had been put forward. For the time being, the Compromise of 1850 stabilized the situation. California entered the Union as a free state. Territorial governments were provided for the rest of the former Mexican lands without any restriction on slavery. A new and harsher law for the return of fugitive slaves was to be enacted and the federal government would not interfere in the interstate slave trade. Because this was a moderate compromise, neither pro- nor anti-slavery lobbies were happy with it, and it looked as if the issue of slavery in the expanding territories of the United States was still a long way from a final solution.

However, the territories were not the only target for anti-slavers. In 1833 the various religious and reforming groups who wanted the complete abolition of slavery thoughout the United States found some degree of national organization through the establishment of the American Anti-Slavery Society. By 1840 2000 local anti-slavery societies, with about 200,000 members, stretched across the Northern States. The leaders of the anti-slavery movement included men such as Benjamin Lundy, a Quaker from New Jersey, and Theodore Dwight Weld, from New York. Perhaps the most famous name was that of William Lloyd Garrison, who wrote that his oppositon to slavery would be 'as harsh as truth and as uncompromising as justice'. Abolitionists were a very active and intellectually powerful minority.

The abolitionist tactic of trying to persuade the Southerners that slavery was immoral and degrading to both slave and owner, was predictably unsuccessful. Therefore the abolitionists concentrated on building up anti-slavery opinion in the North. This was not as easy as it might sound. Dislike of the social institution of slavery amongst Northerners was not the same thing as sympathy for either negroes or radical abolitionism. Indeed there was considerable race hatred among Northerners, and one reason why some Northerners opposed the extension of slavery in the territories was to keep negroes out. In 1837 an abolitionist editor called Elijah P. Lovejoy was murdered by a mob in Alton Illinois (Lincoln's home state).

By the 1850s, however, opposition to slavery was gaining ground in the North. This was partly because of the arrogant pretensions of the Southerners, who seemed to want to open the entire United States to slavery. It was also because Northerners did not want to see the continuation of a sectional interest which was *based* on slavery but which was at odds with the North on many other related issues, such as tariffs and states' rights.

The South characteristically but understandably over-reacted to the abolitionists. Even though slave owners were a minority in the South, most Southerners felt that Northern abolitionism was a threat to their way of life. The Southerners had fearful memories of bloody slave rebellions such as the Nat Turner insurrection and claimed that the abolitionists were inciting the slaves to massacre their masters. Moderate Southern propaganda struck back by trying to justify slavery or portray it in an acceptable light. John C. Calhoun even claimed that slavery was a good thing for all concerned. But at the extreme, cheap and nasty end of the scale, Southerners claimed that abolitionists wanted to 'mongrelize' the human race and merely lusted after 'free love' with black women. By the end of the 1850s neither North nor South seemed able to hear the *moderate* arguments of the opposing section. Northerners seemed to think that all Southerners were arrogant aristocratic slave owners. Most Southerners seemed to think that all the 'damn Yankees' and 'greasy mechanicals' of the North were intent on radical abolitionism and the subjugation of the South.

* * *

When Abraham Lincoln rose to national prominence in the 1850s, civil war in America was not inevitable. However, the United States was divided. The more populous and prosperous North tended to disapprove of slavery and believe that the federal congress could, on the whole, impose its will on all states, for the good of all. The Southerners, who wanted slavery but feared that the numerically dominant Northerners would suppress the interests of the South, tended to emphasize the rights of individual states within the federal union.

In 1831 Turner led a revolt by 50 slaves in Southampton County, Virginia. Fifty-five Whites were murdered and 17 Negroes, including Turner, were hanged.

At first, Southerners were apologetic about slavery, but became more assertive as they were forced to take up defensive positions.

Interpretations

Pioneer Origins and a False Start in Politics

Moving west

The story of the early life of Abraham Lincoln is the story of the westward movement of the frontier during the first half of the nineteenth century. It is also a story in which myth and hearsay sometimes take the place of hard evidence. This is because Lincoln's political supporters in later years wished to portray him as a trustworthy, self-made pioneer endowed with practical wisdom, while his enemies wanted to make him appear a rustic, disreputable hick from the backwoods.

This is what Lincoln himself had to say about his early life, speaking to John Locke Scripps, a sympathetic Republican journalist, in 1860:

> . . . it is a great piece of folly to attempt to make anything out of my early life. It can be all condensed into a simple sentence, and that sentence you will find in Gray's Elegy, "The short and simple annals of the poor". That's my life and that's all you or anyone else can make out of it.

Abraham Lincoln was born on 12 February 1809 at Nolin Creek, Kentucky. His mother, Nancy Hanks, was illiterate and may also have been illegitimate, although there is no conclusive proof. His father was Thomas Lincoln, whose family came from Pennsylvania, but had moved first to Virginia and then westwards to Kentucky as the Frontier advanced. One view of Thomas Lincoln is that he was a drifting, shiftless pioneer, 'unfit for life even in the half-settled society which kept growing up around him'. However, there is a more sympathetic view:

> Throughout his residence in Kentucky Thomas Lincoln was a decent, respected, though far from prominent citizen. He had credit with merchants and paid his bills; he served on juries and in other public capacities; he owned livestock, and supported his little family as well as other men of his station in life.
> P.M. Angle (ed.), *The Lincoln Reader*, Greenwood Press, 1947.

In 1816 the Lincoln family moved to Spencer County, Indiana, keeping

Lincoln was embarrassed by his origins; he worked hard to escape them. But what other reasons may he have had for withholding information to a journalist?

Thomas's early restlessness was probably caused by disputes over the title to his land.

D.W. Brogan, *Abraham Lincoln*, Duckwork 1935.

'From log cabin . . .' the somewhat refurbished birthplace of Abraham Lincoln, Nolin Creek, Kentucky.

pace with the movement of the frontier. Two years later, in the sparsely settled forest of Indiana, Nancy Lincoln died of the 'milk sick'. This possibly set off Lincoln's morbid obsession with mortality and melancholy which was to return to him periodically throughout his life. Thomas Lincoln remarried in 1818, and Abraham grew fond of his step-mother and also of his older sister Sarah. Both women strove hard to fill the gap left by the death of the family's natural mother. In 1828 Abraham worked a flat boat down the Mississippi to New Orleans; this was also the year of Andrew Jackson's Presidential victory, and the Lincolns were Jacksonian Democrats.

The return of the 'milk sick' to Indiana in 1830 may have been the reason for Thomas Lincoln deciding upon another move. An equally important motive may have been the promise of better land available as the frontier moved through Illinois. Thus the Lincoln family arrived in Sangamon County, central Illinois, with a horse, a wagon and four oxen.

Abraham Lincoln was now 21. What had he been like in his childhood and teenage years? Brogan wrote:

> Many legends have grown up about his precocious interest in learning, but in truth, reading fascinated him. He was lazy, where his father was merely shiftless; he would rather talk or recite or read than work; but his amicability and charm secured tolerance for his eccentricities from everyone except his father . . .

Lincoln may not have liked physical toil but there is plenty of evidence that he *was* capable of hard work. Ward Hill Lamon, a lawyer and circuit partner of Lincoln, wrote, 'Any family was glad when "Abe Linkern" was hired to work with them; for he did his work well, and made them all merry . . .'. However, a liking for knowledge, reading and ideas might well have marked him out in the life of the frontier. Certainly Lincoln's formal schooling was very limited, but he undoubtedly encountered a range of reading material including *Robinson Crusoe*, *Pilgrim's Progress*, the Bible and *Bailey's Etymological Dictionary*. In particular he read the early history of the United States and developed a veneration for the Founding Fathers. What was most important was that he was interested in words, ideas and communication. This was his own account:

> I never went to school more than six months in my life, but I can say this: that among my earliest recollections I remember how, when a mere child, I used to get irritated when anybody talked to me in a way I could not understand . . . I could not sleep although I tried to, when I got on such a hunt for an idea until I had caught it; and when I thought I had got it, I was not satisfied until I had repeated it over and over; until I had put it in language plain enough, as I thought, for any boy I knew to comprehend.
> Quoted in S.B. Oates, *With Malice Towards None*, George Allen & Unwin, 1977.

The young man
From 1830 until his marriage in 1842 Lincoln lived the rough-and-tumble life of a young man on the frontier. In 1831 he built a flat boat in the company of his cousin John Hanks and sailed it down the river system to New Orleans. It was quite usual to transport goods by this method and then sell or abandon the flat boat rather than face the long haul back against the strong currents of the Mississippi. In New Orleans Lincoln first came across the horrors of slavery:

> He saw 'negroes in chains – whipped and scourged'. Against this inhumanity his sense of right and justice rebelled, and his mind and conscience were awakened to

Flat boat: a raft-like construction which drifted on the river currents and was guided by steering oars (see illustration on p. 20).

In adulthood Lincoln became estranged from his father.

Lincoln's plain speaking and clear thinking were political assets in later life, but is he himself adding to the legend in this passage?

A Mississippi flat boat. The great rivers of the interior were vital to communication and settlement. Lincoln tried his hand as a flat-boatman.

a realization of what he had often heard and read.
Quoted in Tarbell, *The Life of Abraham Lincoln*, Vol. I.

Lincoln and his fellows also witnessed a slave auction:

These episodes were reported by William Herndon, Lincoln's legal partner and protegé. He may have been myth-building and is not always reliable. He cites Hanks as his source, but Hanks did not reach New Orleans on this trip, turning back at St Louis.

The whole thing was so revolting that Lincoln moved away from the scene with a deep feeling of 'unconquerable hate'. Bidding his companions follow him, he said: 'Boys, let's get away from this. If ever I get a chance to hit that thing' [meaning slavery], 'I'll hit it hard.'

Returning to Illinois, Lincoln became a store clerk in New Salem (which had the grand total of 15 houses at that time). He knocked around with a rowdy group of young men known as the Clary Grove Boys and was respected for his ability to wrestle. However, his employer went out of business and so Lincoln stood as a candidate for election to the State Legislature, but was unsuccessful. During this period he also gained military experience as a militia captain in the Black Hawk Indian War. He may have been a good natural leader, but was not good at orthodox soldiering and was made to wear a wooden sword as punishment for the disorderliness of his company.

In 1832 about a thousand Sac and Fox Indians resisted the policy of moving them westwards and returned to Illinois. The army and the militia easily defeated them.

His next venture was a partnership in a general store, which according to Lincoln 's political enemies chiefly sold alcoholic liquor. Losing money on the store, the partners sold out, but the new owners ran off and left Lincoln to cover a $1100 debt (his partner having died in the meantime). Accounts vary, but Lincoln took between 15 and 20 years to pay off the debt; the fact that he paid up instead of disappearing is usually mentioned to his credit.

Meanwhile, Lincoln had already taken up additional work as a postmaster and as a surveyor. The two jobs could be combined, as he rode around the county with letters and plans tucked away in his stove-pipe hat. Nicolay and Hay report that he was well known and well respected – strong but gentle, humorous but wise and the subject of many remarkable anecdotes, one of which claimed he had lifted a box of stones weighing half a ton!

It was easy to 'disappear' in the shifting society of the Frontier; a man who moved on would be difficult to trace.

1834 saw him elected to the State Legislature with the support of all parties, although he was actually a Clay Whig, favouring high tariffs and internal improvements. In the State Legislature he had his first encounters with his life-long Democratic rival, Stephen A. Douglas. He also participated in removing the state capital from Vandalia to Springfield, and denounced slavery, although he also denounced abolitionism for good measure. Lincoln did not like slavery but he was never an outright abolitionist either. Slavery was legal, and as a politician and lawyer Lincoln could not be seen to support the abolitionists since they frequently broke the law in helping Blacks to escape.

Suffrage: the right to vote.

In fact, in the legislative session of 1835-36 he'd voted in favour of restricting the suffrage to white only. Public opinion was almost universally against political rights for black people, and young Lincoln, who had elected to work within the system, was not about to ruin his career by supporting Negro suffrage. Nor was he going to get himself branded as an abolitionist, because in Sangemon County that would be certain political suicide.
Oates, *With Malice Towards None*.

Oates is drawing a far more complex picture of Lincoln's approach to the slavery issue than the earlier account from Herndon.

Inquorate: lacking sufficient members present to make any official decisions.

In the Legislature Lincoln developed his oratorical skills, but also learned some tactical skills as well; to prevent a vote being taken he made a session inquorate by climbing out of the window!

While all this was going on, Lincoln was studying law, and he was admitted to the Illinois Bar in 1836. He now had a suitable profession for a politician!

Marriage

The young Abraham Lincoln seems to have been awkward in the company of women. A number of stories have arisen about his troublesome romantic involvements, and some of them seem to be untrue in the light of recent investigations. The first involves Ann Rutledge, whom he came to know in New Salem. It is said that he fell in love with her, and that when she died of 'brain fever' in 1835 his heart was 'buried with her'. But it was unlikely that Ann was the 'only woman that he ever loved'. The evidence seems to suggest that their friendship was warm but platonic.

The woman that he married was Mary Todd. She was an attractive, educated and rather hot-tempered member of a distinguished Kentucky family. She was ambitious, and it seemed strange that she should choose the tall, awkward young lawyer, when her suitors included the dynamic 'Little Giant' Stephen A. Douglas. It seemed strange to Lincoln too, who according to one story left her stranded at the altar on the occasion of their first attempt to get married. This story is probably not true; no marriage

Mary Lincoln with her favourite hairstyle. 'She terrorized housemaids, icemen, storekeepers, delivery boys, with her tongue lashings.' She usually looks very hard in photographs, but this is a more sympathetic portrayal (taken by Brady in Washington D.C.).

licence was taken out by Lincoln in the relevant year. However, they *did* split up and then come together again, to get married in November 1842.

The traditional story is that Mary made their domestic life hell and that the marriage was a disaster: David Donald gives this account of the once generally accepted story (which he subsequently goes on to refute):

> . . . Lincoln's life was a domestic hell. Mary made it so unpleasant for him that he was forced to interest himself in politics. He was driven from home into the White House.
> David Donald, *Lincoln Reconsidered*, Greenwood Press, 1956.

Donald traces this view of the Lincoln marriage back to Lincoln's legal partner, William Herndon. He argues that the story really originates from Herndon's own inability to get on with Mary, whom he had accidentally offended at their first meeting. Herndon's own family life was so settled that he could not understand why Lincoln could spend months away from home practising law on the Illinois state circuit. Herndon concluded, falsely according to Donald, that it must have been Mary Lincoln's fault. It is true that the Lincoln marriage had its stormy moments, for Mary had fits of temper and a terrible fear of falling into poverty, and Lincoln had his bouts of melancholy. But Donald concludes that the marriage was essentially stable and successful. Nevertheless, once Herndon's version was made public in 1865 there was no shortage of 'witnesses' who could testify to the shouting matches that the Lincolns were supposed to have had. Among Mary's fiercest critics were Nicolay and Hay, Lincoln's wartime secretaries at the White House and his first official biographers; they called her a 'hellcat' and did not understand the strains that existed between Abraham and Mary Lincoln over money, his involvement in public life, long hours of work and the confidentiality of affairs of state.

By early 1865, Mary Lincoln had run up debts of $27,000, slightly more than Lincoln's annual salary as President.

Eddie (1846-50) died after a long illness and Willie (1850-62) died of fever. Two other sons, Robert (born in 1843) and Tad (Thomas, born in 1853) outlived their father.

Poor Mary Lincoln; having suffered the deaths of two of her sons and the assassination of her husband she had to listen to Herndon's assassination of her own character. She was to die a recluse, living in the candlelight of a shuttered room of the Lincoln family home on the corner of Eighth and Jackson Streets, Springfield, Illinois.

Frustrated ambition and personal tragedy

Lincoln's political career during the period 1841 to 1846 was fairly uneventful, although he was fully immersed in his profession, his home life and the devious ins and outs of Illinois Whig politics. Eventually, having awaited his turn, he was nominated for the federal House of Representatives. Duly elected, he arrived in Washington in the middle of the political turmoil created by President Polk's territorial gains. These were Texas and Oregon (gained by negotiation) and California (effectively the whole Pacific South-West, gained by war from Mexico). Congress had to decide the basis on which these new lands would be organized into territories, and the biggest problem was whether or not slavery should be allowed in them.

Lincoln was now thoroughly convinced that slavery was wrong and therefore he supported the 'free soilers' who wanted to prevent the extension of slavery in the newly acquired territories. He claimed that in the session of 1848-9 he voted at least 40 times for the free-soil Wilmot Proviso. Lincoln even went so far as informing the House of Representatives that he intended to introduce a bill to outlaw slavery in the District of Columbia (the federal territory in which Washington is situated), but the hostility which this provoked was too great for the obscure and lonely Congressman from Illinois, and the bill did not appear. Lincoln was well aware that

See p. 16.

The corner of Eighth and Jackson, Lincoln's home in Springfield, Illinois. Lincoln stands within the fence, but who is that with him?

slavery was a complex and potentially disastrous issue, and much as he hated slavery he understood that it would be very difficult to both abolish slavery *and* keep Americans united:

Lincoln's oft-quoted habit of telling humorous stories annoyed some of his more stuffy political supporters, but the habit had its uses!

When such conversation [about slavery] would threaten angry or even unpleasant contention he would interrupt it by interposing some anecdote, thus diverting it into a hearty and general laugh . . .
A Congressional colleague, quoted in Tarbell, *The Life of Abraham Lincoln*, Vol. I 1895.

The abolitionists, well aware that as yet Congress did not possess the power to abolish slavery in the states, believed that either moral persuasion or direct action could be employed to bring about the abolition of slavery as rapidly as possible. Lincoln, however, was more realistic and saw that constitutional progress against slavery could only be achieved one small step at a time.

The most obvious form of direct action was to assist fugitive slaves; forms of political action were limited to seeking the abolition of slavery in the District of Columbia and in the territories.

For all this, Lincoln's career in national politics still ended up on the scrap heap by the end of 1848. He joined in the Whig Party's condemnation of Polk for deliberately provoking the Mexican War and misleading Congress in the process. As a result, Lincoln angered his constituents back in Illinois, most of whom, as Westerners, supported any policy which extended the territory of the United States. Illinois did not elect Lincoln for a second two-year term in the House of Representatives. Indeed the year of 1848 dealt him a double blow. He worked hard on the successful campaign

The Lincoln family in 1861 (showing similarities to certain photographs). Robert in the background, Abraham, Willie, Tad and Mary left to right.

to get Zachary Taylor, hero of the Mexican War, elected as President. Taylor had no other asset than his military achievements in a war that the Whigs had condemned, but such was the way of American politics that the Whigs chose him and won with him. Unfortunately, Lincoln won nothing. Like many other hopefuls who had toed the national party line, he expected to be rewarded with a job in the federal administration. The American political system works in such a way that the election of a new President is followed by a rush for the jobs and favours that are in the gift of the new chief executive. But Lincoln was only offered the secretaryship of the Oregon Territory. This was a minor post, and he refused it. He returned home to Illinois depressed, disillusioned with politics and with no real alternative but to concentrate on his law practice. This was a really difficult time for the Lincolns. In 1850 their son Eddie died, adding to the bouts of melancholic depression or 'hypo' from which Lincoln suffered. To make things worse, although there was a Whig in the White House, the party itself was dying on its feet. In 1852 the Whigs put up another Mexican War hero, Winfield Scott, for the Presidency, but the trick did not work twice. This was the fatal blow to the Whig party.

Privately ambitious despite his outward modesty, Lincoln must have watched ruefully the growing success of rivals. Stephen A. Douglas was by this time riding high in the Democratic Party. He was a member of the Senate and amassing a fortune in railroad speculation. Yet, ironically, it was Douglas who rocked national and local politics and set in chain the tenuous series of events which led Lincoln back from obscurity to the White House.

Return to Politics 1854-8

The lawyer

In the early 1850s Lincoln was living the life of a Frontier lawyer. Twice a year he followed Judge David Davis around the route of the Eighth Illinois Circuit Court. He rode in a horse-drawn rig with his belongings in a carpet bag. He lived in rough and crowded hotels, sharing beds with his fellow circuit court lawyers and yarning long in to the night once the day's work was over. His humorous anecdotes and country style wisdom were sought after, especially by Judge Davis himself, who became a key Lincoln supporter. Indeed, it turned out that the chief value of following the circuit lay in making political contacts.

For the rest of the year Lincoln practised law from his hometown of Springfield. He appeared in the federal courts, the Illinois Supreme Court, and on two occasions, the Supreme Court of the United States.

What sort of lawyer was Lincoln? Characteristically, he understated his own ability:

I am not an accomplished lawyer. I find quite as much material for a lecture in those points wherein I have failed, as in those where I have been moderately successful.
Quoted in Oates, *With Malice Towards None*.

Certainly Lincoln's office routine was haphazard. He did some of his office work lying on an old sofa; the Lincoln boys were indulgently allowed to play unchecked among the legal papers. But Brogan's summary of Lincoln's ability puts things in a different light: 'He was an excellent lawyer with a good case, a poor one with a bad case.' The facts of the matter seem to be

The earliest known photograph of Lincoln, taken in Springfield, Illinois, in 1846 – distinctive to say the least, with huge hands and at least one large ear.

This remark was addressed to an audience; how should it be regarded?

Lincoln the Lawyer. Abraham Lincoln in action in the old courthouse, Shelbyville, Illinois, 15 June 1856.

that Lincoln was good at appealing to frontier juries and at carefully presenting a case before the more leisured higher courts. He had a certain fascination with the technical details of patent cases; he even used models to illustrate his points. However, in the eyes of smart eastern attorneys he was still a hick country lawyer. When he was hired in a patent case to give local support to Edwin Stanton (a Pennsylvanian, and later Lincoln's Secretary of War) Lincoln was treated with arrogant scorn.

Part of the Lincoln mythology portrays him as the honest, selfless defender of the oppressed poor. On one occasion he defended a widow who was being cheated of her pension. In 1841 he persuaded the Illinois Supreme Court that it should free a negro girl sold by one white man to another, on the grounds that slavery was outlawed in Illinois under the terms of the North-West Ordinance of 1787. It was true that Lincoln would undertake such jobs as these, and if necessary he would do such work free of charge. Even so, a more balanced picture of Lincoln the lawyer has long been available:

In 1847 Lincoln appeared on behalf of a Kentucky slave owner trying to recover his runaway property.

He was honest – notoriously so – free from the pettier tricks of the trade, but not the modern whimsical Saint Francis of legend, going about doing good, careless of reward. He appeared on both sides of most questions, even of the slavery question, although he was notoriously opposed to slavery. He argued for and against rich clients. He lived up to the highest standards of his profession, but not beyond them. Brogan, *Abraham Lincoln.*

Lincoln could make $5,000 for appearing on behalf of the Illinois Central Railroad; the law made him comfortably well off, well-known, and generally respected in Illinois. Even so, the attractions of politics still pulled at him strongly. Lincoln had kept in touch with his Whig political contacts, but what gave him his great new opportunity was the national debate and re-alignment of political parties provoked by Stephen Douglas's Kansas-Nebraska Bill.

Rebirth: The Kansas-Nebraska Bill

The Kansas-Nebraska Bill was the first of a series of crises during the 1850s which revolved around Slavery. Each crisis left the defenders of slavery believing more firmly that the opponents of slavery intended its destruction throughout the Union (although the majority of moderate anti-slavers only expected to restrict its spread). On the other hand, the opponents of slavery

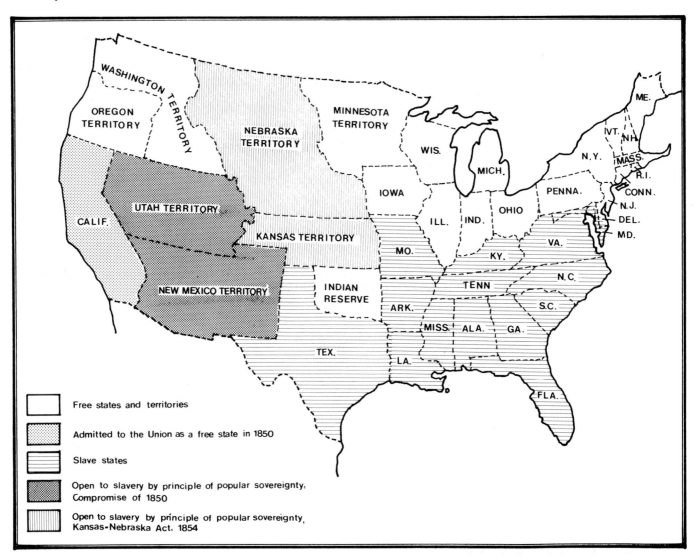

Free states and territories

Admitted to the Union as a free state in 1850

Slave states

Open to slavery by principle of popular sovereignty, Compromise of 1850

Open to slavery by principle of popular sovereignty, Kansas-Nebraska Act, 1854

The Kansas-Nebraska Act, 1854.

Railroads had already reached as far west as the Mississippi, but now that the lands possessed by the United States stretched as far as the Pacific, great economic opportunities existed for the promoters of the first railroad to reach the west coast.

increasingly believed that its supporters would not be satisfied until slavery was allowed across the entire Union. It was these entrenched beliefs of slavers and anti-slavers that eventually produced civil war.

In 1854 Stephen A. Douglas, Senator for Illinois and Chairman of the Senate Committee on the Territories, introduced a Bill to organize the northern part of the Louisiana Purchase into two territories: Kansas and Nebraska. This was so that the area could proceed towards the formation of territorial governments and then enter into the Union as a number of separate states. Douglas had two main motives. The first was that he wanted to build up his reputation ready to secure the Democratic nomination for the next presidential election. The second was that he wanted to secure the success of a proposed transcontinental railroad running from Chicago (in his home state), through Nebraska and Utah, to the west coast. To achieve this, and to beat rival schemes in the South, he wanted to extinguish Indian claims in Nebraska and encourage the settlement of potential railroad users as rapidly as possible.

What made the Kansas-Nebraska Bill so controversial was its provision for slavery in these new territories. The situation so far was that the Missouri Compromise of 1820 said that slavery was not allowed north of 36°30′. But the Compromise of 1850 said that in Utah and New Mexico territories, much of which lay *north* of 36°30′, the issue of whether or not to have slavery should be decided upon by the inhabitants. But Kansas and Nebraska were at one and the same time both north of 36°30′ and level with part of New Mexico and all of Utah. Could slavery be allowed in Kansas and Nebraska? Douglas's answer, in his bill, was Yes; he proposed to repeal the Missouri Compromise and to allow the principle of popular sovereignty which existed in New Mexico and Utah to rule in Kansas and Nebraska as well, making slavery possible there if the new settlers wanted it.

Popular sovereignty: the idea that the power of decision should rest with the people.

Douglas was perhaps surprised at the fury which his proposals aroused among anti-slavers. He failed to realize how much of a moral issue slavery had become. Lincoln later accused Douglas of being part of a wicked pro-slavery plot to extend servitude to all corners of the United States, but this was probably not true. Douglas was a man of greater integrity and less enthusiasm for slavery than most of the Lincoln biographies suggest, but his vested interests in the transcontinental railroad scheme made him into a man in a hurry. To be sure of getting the Kansas-Nebraska Bill through Congress he needed the support of the Southern slave states and also of Missouri. Missouri was itself a slave state, which would be very hostile to the existence of a free Kansas in its immediate backyard. The way to get the necessary support from Missouri and the Southern states was to open Kansas and Nebraska to slavery. The Kansas-Nebraska Bill became law in May 1854 with the strong backing of the Democratic President, Franklin Pierce.

Douglas was, in fact, of the opinion that slavery was not an economic proposition in Kansas or Nebraska.

Consequences of the Kansas-Nebraska Act

Many prominent politicians opposed the Kansas-Nebraska Act, including Sumner of Massachusetts and Chase of Ohio. The effect of the Act was to split both the ruling Democratic Party and the ailing Whig Party along broadly sectional lines (that is between slavers and anti-slavers). 'Free-Soil' Democrats, 'anti-Nebraska' Democrats, 'conscience' Whigs and various other anti-slavery groups met in Jackson, Michigan, to form the Republican Party. The Republicans claimed to be the descendants of the Jeffersonians, and wanted slavery to be contained within those states where it already existed. They opposed the doctrine of popular sovereignty as applied to Kansas and Nebraska by Douglas. Abolitionism was never part of the party policy, but many Republicans hoped that eventually slavery would die out completely in the United States. However, although the bulk of the Republicans were essentially moderate, slavers believed that the

Charles Sumner helped found the Free-Soil Party and was a Senator for Massachusetts. Salmon P. Chase was a founder of the Free-Soil party, a Senator and then from 1855, governor of Ohio. Both later became Republicans, and Chase served in Lincoln's cabinet as Secretary of the Treasury.

What Stephen Douglas may have thought the Kansas-Nebraska Act was about – the Union Pacific Railroad depot at Omaha Nebraska (probably some time after 1861).

John Brown was an abolitionist who believed in the need for a slave insurrection. In 1855 he joined his five sons at Ossawatomie in Kansas and deliberately planned and carried out the massacre of the five supporters of slavery.

Republican intention was to destroy slavery, even if this was not openly stated; to Southerners it was the 'Black Republican Party' of the North.

The outcome of the Kansas-Nebraska Act in Nebraska was peaceful settlement and slavery was not allowed, but in Kansas it was guerilla warfare. Pro-slavery settlers from Missouri, and Free-Soilers, many with Eastern help, rushed to occupy Kansas and decide, according to popular sovereignty, whether or not there should be slavery. Two territorial governments were formed: the official government was pro-slavery but based on fraudulent elections, and the unofficial government was anti-slavery and based on fairer elections. Neither side would yield. It only required the interference of extremists to bring about bloodshed. John Brown advocated the use of armed force against slavery. He retaliated against intimidation by Missourians by killing five settlers at Pottawatomie Creek. The preacher Henry Ward Beecher said that Sharps rifles were more effective against slavery than was the Bible, and so 'Beecher's Bibles' opened fire as well. Range war had begun. Meanwhile, two rival constitutions for Kansas were seeking Congressional approval. The Lecompton Constitution would allow slavery, but the rival Topeka Constitution would allow neither slavery nor free Blacks to enter Kansas (outright abolitionists were a minority of one in three among Free-Soilers). By 1856 the Kansas issue became so heated that charles Sumner was beaten unconscious at his desk in the Senate. Was 'Bleeding Kansas' the way that the United States was headed?

Lincoln and Kansas-Nebraska

Lincoln was deeply opposed to the Kansas-Nebraska Act – in 1859 he wrote in a letter to a friend, 'I was losing interest in politics when the repeal of the Missouri Compromise aroused me again'. But he may also have seen the Act as a set of political circumstances on which he could rebuild his political career. Was this a matter of principle or of opportunism? He had certainly become more involved in his legal work since his 'retirement' from politics, but, on the other hand, had stayed in contact with the Whig Party machine in Illinois and it is perhaps difficult to believe that Lincoln's ambition – that 'little engine that knew no rest', to quote Herndon – had completely run out of steam.

There is no reason to doubt the sincerity of Lincoln's opposition to the extension of slavery made possible by the Kansas-Nebraska Act. Yet his views on slavery were complex. He believed that slavery was a moral wrong. He also believed that the Founding Fathers had intended that slavery should eventually be extinguished in the United States. His evidence for this was that the Declaration of Independence said that, 'all men are created equal'. He believed that this was certainly true in the sense that all men have the right to life, liberty and the enjoyment of property. He also cited the North-West Territorial Ordinance of 1787 as evidence of the Founding Fathers' intentions, for this forbade the extension of slavery into such unsettled territories as then existed.

In the Lincoln mythology he is the friend of the slaves, but his attitude to Blacks would probably nowadays be called racist. He did not believe that Blacks and Whites were capable of living on terms of social, economic or intellectual equality in America as it then existed. In the early part of his career he opposed the granting of voting rights to Blacks in Illinois. He was, in effect, a white supremacist of a humane sort. Thus:

When it is said that the institution [of slavery] exists and that it is very difficult to get rid of it in any satisfactory way, I can appreciate and understand the saying

. . . . My first impulse would be to free all the slaves and send them to Liberia – to their own native land. But a moment's reflection would convince me that whatever of high hope (as I think there is) there may be in this, in the long run, its sudden execution is impossible . . . . What next? Free them, and make them politically and socially our equals? My own feelings would not admit of this; and if mine would, we well know that the great mass of white people will not.
From Lincoln's speech in Ottawa, Illinois, 1858.

This view would nowadays be regarded by many people as unrealistic and wholly unsympathetic to the way in which the slaves had developed their own Afro-American culture.

He stuck to the belief that if slavery could be prevented from spreading it would eventually die out. But in the meantime it would have to be tolerated because it was neither constitutionally nor practically possible to get rid of it. He pinned his faith on the power of rational persuasion:

Let there be peace. In a democracy, where a majority rule by the ballot through the forms of law, these physical rebellions and bloody resistances are radically wrong, unconstitutional, and are treason. Better bear the ills you have than to fly to those you know not of. Our own Declaration of Independence says that the government long established, for trivial causes should not be resisted. Revolutionize through the ballot-box, and restore the government once more to the affections and hearts of men, by making it express, as it was intended to do, the highest spirit of justice and liberty.
Speech by Lincoln at Springfield, Illinois, to a delegation intending to visit Kansas Territory in the physical defence of freedom.

He also believed that it would be necessary for the federal government to compensate the former slave owners.

The essential point about Lincoln's views on slavery is that *by the standards of his day* he was both moderate and humane. But perhaps it is no surprise that supporters of slavery thought that his moderation was disingenuous, and that, 'earnest antislavery men were wary of him – or worse . . .'.

David Donald, *Lincoln Reconsidered.*

Thus Lincoln believed that the Kansas-Nebraska Act, with its repeal of the Missouri Compromise, was a revolt against the aims of the Founding Fathers. He resumed his public political career in the summer of 1854. It was congressional election time, and Douglas was stumping Illinois attempting to overcome the opposition in his home state to the Kansas-Nebraska Act. In October, Douglas spoke at the rain-lashed State Fair in Springfield, and the day after, Lincoln replied. There followed a series of public exchanges which ended in Douglas crying 'enough', for the time being. The key Lincoln speeches were at Springfield and at Peoria. What strikes the twentieth-century reader is the high intellectual level of these addresses to mass audiences. The text of the Springfield speech does not exist, but it is believed to have been basically the same as that delivered at Peoria, which *is* on the record.

Stumping: campaigning or canvassing.

Lincoln said that the Kansas-Nebraska Act was wrong because it betrayed the Declaration of Independence and it broke the great Missouri Compromise of 1820. He said he hated the Act because he hated, 'the monstrous injustice of slavery itself'. He claimed that the continuation of slavery allowed the enemies of liberty and republicanism to call Americans hypocrites. The survival of slavery caused the friends of liberty to doubt the sincerity of Americans. Even so, he expressed moderation and even generosity and understanding towards 'our bretheren of the South':

Lincoln's attitude expressed here was to become characteristic. Sympathetic historians regard it as a sign of statesmanship, moderation and human understanding. But how do you think abolitionists, or Southerners, might view these sentiments?

[The Southerners] are just what we would be in their situation . . . . If it [slavery] did now exist among us [Northerners], we should not instantly give it up . . . I surely will not blame them for not doing what I should not know how to do myself.

In the Springfield and Peoria speeches Lincoln went on to deal with the doctrine of popular sovereignty, or as he referred to it, 'self-government'.

The doctrine of self-government is right . . . but it has no just application as here attempted [in the Kansas-Nebraska Act] . . . When the white man governs himself, that is self-government; but when he governs himself and also governs another man, that is more than self-government – that is despotism. If the negro is a man, why then my ancient faith tells me that, 'all men are created equal,' and that there can be no moral right in connection with one man's making a slave of another.

The argument was already moving in the direction of asking, 'who has the right to decide whether or not to have slavery?' Lincoln's view was that the extension of slavery was too great an issue to be decided on at a local level by popular sovereignty. It had to be decided at a national level by the federal government. Congress should forbid slavery in the territories.

According to the *Springfield Journal*, Lincoln was speaking from the heart:

He felt upon his soul the truths burn which he uttered, and all present felt he was true to his own soul. His feelings once or twice swelled within, and came near to stifling utterance.

Quoted in Tarbell, *The Life of Abraham Lincoln*, Vol. I

Sincerity? What reliance should one put on this extract?

In November 1854 Lincoln became a successful candidate for the State Legislature of Illinois. Lincoln followed this up by making his first attempt to become a United States senator; he failed, but nevertheless was able to assist in the election of another anti-Nebraska man, Trumbull, to the Senate in Washington.

As yet, Lincoln was still a member of the Whig Party. The new Republican Party was attractive to him, but he was cautious about abandoning the Whigs; their decline was less obvious at the time than it is to historians with the benefit of hindsight. But by 1856, the former Whig, William Seward, Senator for New York, and the former Democrat, Salmon P. Chase, Governor of Ohio, had joined the Republicans. With prominent national figures such as these staking their political careers on the new party, Lincoln was prepared to risk his more local reputation as well.

Each state is represented in the United States Senate (the upper house of Congress) by two senators. In Lincoln's day, Senators were chosen by the numbers of the legislature of each state and so it was the elections to the *State* Legislature which were the crucial contest.

In May 1856, Lincoln was instrumental in arranging a meeting of anti-Nebraska forces in Bloomington Illinois. As news came in of massacres in Kansas and the caning of Sumner, the decision was taken to create a branch of the Republican Party in Illinois. Lincoln gave the keynote address, a triumph of oratory but not recorded, and therefore known as the 'Lost Speech'. But at least the journalist Joseph Medill remembered how he came to forget the exact text of what was said against Douglas and the policies of the Democrats:

I well remember that after Lincoln sat down and calm had succeeded the tempest, I waked out of a sort of hypnotic trance . . . all the newspaper men present had been equally carried away by the excitement caused by the wonderful oration and had made no report or sketch of the speech.

Quoted in Tarbell, *The Life of Abraham Lincoln*, Lincoln, Vol. I.

'Myth-making' again? Herndon and others later reported that they were similarly carried away. But an account of the speech *was* published in 1896, based on the notes of H.C. Whitney, a lawyer on Lincoln's circuit.

The Lincoln-Douglas Debates

In the Presidential election of 1856 the Republican Party, in its first contest, came second to the Democrats in a three-cornered fight. The Republican candidate was John C. Frémont, a popular explorer and opponent of slavery. His slogan was, 'Free Soil, Free Speech and Frémont'; the policy was: no extension of slavery in the territories. The successful Democratic

Douglas did not stand in the election, Kansas-Nebraska had cost him the nomination.

The issue which actually brought civil war about in 1861 was already in circulation.

Taney and four other judges were from slave states. How might the judgment be viewed?

candidate was James Buchanan, fighting on a platform which said that the federal government had no right to decide whether or not a territory could have slavery.

The campaign was marked by exaggeration on both sides. Democratic propaganda said that if the Republicans won, the South would be forced to secede from the Union, because the truth of it was that the Republicans were abolitionists. Lincoln himself replied: 'We won't go out of the Union, and you shan't.' On the other hand, the Republicans depicted Kansas as a paradise being lost to grasping slavery men, although it was never this simple.

The election of Buchanan solved nothing. The United States was suffering from a succession of weak Presidencies. Buchanan had ducked the issues, hoping that the whole problem of slavery in the territories would be solved by the forthcoming decision of the Supreme Court in the Dred Scott case. Buchanan urged all parties to accept this decision as final.

Dred Scott was a slave who had been taken by his master into Missouri, and then to the free state of Illinois. Thence he had been taken to Wisconsin Territory, north of 36° 30', the Missouri Compromise line. He had sued for his freedom in the Missouri courts on the basis that he had been taken into an area closed to slavery by the Missouri Compromise. The case had eventually been taken on appeal to the Supreme Court. The two questions that the Supreme Court had to rule on were: was Scott a citizen of the United States and therefore entitled to sue in the federal courts; and was the Missouri Compromise constitutional in excluding slavery from certain territories?

In 1857 the Supreme Court decided six to three against Scott, and Chief Justice Robert B. Taney gave two judgments which outraged Free-Soilers and abolitionists. In an interpretation of American constitutional history stacked with racism he pronounced that negroes were:

. . . a subordinate and inferior class of beings, who had been subjugated by the dominant race, and . . . remained subject to their authority.
Quoted in H.S. Commager, *Documents of American History*, Appleton-Century-Crafts Inc., 1938.

Taney's first conclusion was, therefore, that a negro could *not* be a citizen of the United States. He then went on to state that slaves were property and that under the Constitution a citizen could not be deprived of his property 'without due process of law'. Banning slavery north of 36° 30' amounted to depriving slave owners of their property; therefore the Missouri Compromise had been unconstitutional. This final part of the judgment was the absolute bombshell, because in plain terms it meant that Congress had no power to forbid slavery in the territories; the territories were *open* to slavery, and only a state could forbid it.

Taney's judgment was open to serious legal and practical doubts, and of course there was no chance that the Republican Party would accept the Dred Scott verdict as final. Lincoln took up the fight by attacking Douglas. In 1858 Lincoln challenged his life-long political rival from Illinois for his seat in the Senate. The election campaign became famous for the series of public debates between Lincoln and Douglas on the matter of slavery in the territories. They helped to start a tradition of face-to-face confrontation between rival candidates which has continued in American history through to the television debates of today. Lincoln argued that Congress should ban slavery in the territories; Douglas said that popular sovereignty should decide.

Stephen A Douglas, the 'Little Giant'.

His confidence and aggression may in part have stemmed from the fact that he drank too much; alcohol and the influence of a bad woman was held by many to be the reason for the eventual eclipse of his powers.

There were seven debates, which covered each congressional district of Illinois. They started in the blistering August sunshine and went on into the penetrating wet and cold of autumn on the prairie. The classic image of the debates is that they were duels of words between the fashionably dressed, small, but powerfully built figure of Douglas, and the shambling, untidy but thoughtful and homespun 'Abe' Lincoln. Douglas would travel by his own special train, provided by the Illinois Central Railroad. A cannon shot would announce his arrival, and the 'Little Giant' would be escorted from the railroad depot to the open-air meeting place; he would be exuding confidence and aggression. Then Lincoln would arrive:

On his head he wore a somewhat battered stovepipe hat. His neck emerged, long and sinewy, from a white collar turned down over a thin black necktie. His lank, ungainly body was clad in a rusty black dress coat with sleeves that should have been longer; but his arms appeared so long that the sleeves of a store coat could hardly be expected to cover them all the way down to the wrists. His black trousers, too, permitted a very full view of his large feet. On his left arm he carried a gray woollen shawl, which evidently served him for an overcoat in chilly weather. His left hand held a cotton umbrella of the bulging kind, and also a black satchel that bore the marks of long and hard usage. His right he had kept free for handshaking, of which there was no end until everybody in the car seemed to be satisfied. I had

This account was written by Karl Schurz, meeting Lincoln in Quincy, where the sixth debate was held on 13 October. This passage fully reflects the traditional image of Lincoln, but recent writers such as Oates point out that Lincoln was comfortably well-off financially and his dress, though at times eccentric like the man himself, was probably quite typical of the western lawyer. Douglas's clothes appear to have come from a fashionable Washington tailor.

Lincoln was not religious in a conventional sense, but he was fully capable of using Biblical references. This speech was a warning of the possible fate in store for the USA. It was *not* preaching abolitionism, but nevertheless he hoped that slavery would wither away once it was no longer allowed to spread.

Douglas, Pierce, Taney and Buchanan. This accusation was a great exaggeration. Indeed Douglas was already experiencing differences with his fellow Democrats.

seen, in Washington and in the West, several public men of rough appearance; but none whose looks seemed quite so uncouth, not to say grotesque, as Lincoln's.

There would then follow an exchange of complex political and legal arguments between the two men, addressed to a crowd of perhaps 12-15,000 standing in dust, hot sun or cutting wind. The debates would last for three hours or more, and were conducted, of course, without the benefit of a modern public address system; what a contrast to the modern five-minute party political broadcast, and no wonder that the speakers grew hoarse! But the crowds loved it, for this was great public entertainment, complete with bands, banners, stunts and demonstrations by rival groups of supporters in the home state of the two contenders.

The battle lines were drawn by Lincoln in his famous 'House Divided' speech at Springfield in June of 1858, the occasion of the Illinois Republican Party State Convention at which Lincoln was formally adopted as a candidate for the Senate. Lincoln started by referring to the bloodshed and turmoil caused by the Kansas-Nebraska Act and then said:

In my opinion, it will not cease until a crisis shall have been reached and passed. "A house divided against itself cannot stand". I believe this government cannot endure permanently half slave and half free. I do not expect the Union to be dissolved; I do not expect the house to fall; but I do expect it will cease to be divided. It will become all one thing, or all the other.

He accused the Democrats of a plot to open the whole Union to slavery:

. . . we find it impossible not to believe that Stephen and Franklin and Roger and James all understood one another from the beginning, and all worked on a common plan . . .

Lincoln poured scorn on Douglas's claim that he 'cared not' whether slavery in Kansas were voted 'up' or 'down', but only that the doctrine of popular sovereignty should triumph. Lincoln clearly believed that Douglas was being either cynically amoral, or just plain dishonest. Lincoln's conclusion was that the Republicans should unite to defeat the Democratic Party's designs.

The first debate took place at Ottawa. Douglas claimed that *he* was on the side of the Founding Fathers, who had created the United States part slave and part free. He alleged that the Republicans' real purpose was abolitionism and to stir up civil war; they intended to make negroes the political and social equals of whites. Lincoln replied that the Republicans did *not* intend to try to abolish slavery where it already existed and that he did *not* regard negroes as his intellectual or social equals; nor indeed did he believe that free negroes in Illinois should have equal civil rights with whites. But he *did* believe that negroes had an equal right to freedom, happiness and the fruits of their own labour. Lincoln again said that Douglas was in reality party to a plot to extend slavery to all of the Union and that there were already covert plans to bring about a Supreme Court judgment which would make it unconstitutional for *state* governments (not just territorial governments) to outlaw slavery. ('A lie' said Douglas.)

The next debate was at Freeport, and its effects were far-reaching. Lincoln went on the offensive and struck at the weak point in Douglas's arguments. The Dred Scott decision said that a territory could not ban slavery, but if this was so then Douglas's doctrine of popular sovereignty was invalid, for the people of the territories had no choice. Douglas replied by saying that the people of the territories could still reject slavery by refusing to enact the police powers necessary to protect it. This was the crucial 'Freeport Doctrine'. It was enough of an answer to win the senatorial election for Douglas, but, as Lincoln was able to point out, it was vague and evasive, a 'chimerical' answer. Worse still from Douglas's point of view, the Freeport Doctrine upset the Southerners in his own party, for they felt that popular sovereignty was no longer a guarantee of the extension of slavery; Douglas was splitting his party and destroying once again his chances of the Democratic nomination for the Presidency.

By challenging Douglas on the implications of the Dred Scott decision Lincoln was running a risk; it gave Douglas a chance, for the time being, to patch up the inconsistences in his argument. But Lincoln seems to have been looking at the longer term: 'I am after a larger game; the battle of 1860 is worth a hundred of this.'

As the debates continued, Lincoln was forced more and more to deal with Douglas's race-baiting. At his most polite, Douglas accused Lincoln of believing in racial equality, and at his most unpleasant he played on the racial fears of those listening by saying that the Republicans wanted intermarriage. Lincoln wanted to debate the *moral* issues of slavery, but was forced to declare that he had never believed in 'making voters or jurors of Negroes, nor of qualifying them to hold office, nor to intermarry with white people.'

In the end, Lincoln's bid for the senatorship failed; seven years from the end of his life and he still had not made it into the 'big time'. But without doubt the Lincoln-Douglas Debates made Lincoln into a nationally known figure. The arguments were reported in the East Coast papers, journalists and editors being attracted by the fame of 'the Little Giant' and by the quality of Lincoln's campaign:

No man of this generation has grown more rapidly before the country than Lincoln in this canvass.
New York Evening Post, quoted in Tarbell, *The Life of Abraham Lincoln*, Vol. I.

Before the Kansas struggle Abraham Lincoln had been distinguished from hundreds of North-Western lawyer-politicians only by a high reputation for integrity and a habit of prolonged, abstracted contemplation.
Morison, Commager and Leuchtenburg, *A Concise History of the American Republic*.

However, the importance of the Lincoln-Douglas Debates should not be exaggerated. Lincoln *had* been heard of before. The Illinois Republican Party had nominated Lincoln to run for the Vice Presidency in 1856. Although the National Convention passed him over he had nevertheless received 110 votes. Nor were his ideas unique. In 1858 the leading Republican, Seward, was saying basically the same things as Lincoln. Most importantly, by running against Douglas, Lincoln was in conflict with all but the Illinois section of the Republicans. This was because the Republicans were hoping to team up with Douglas following his split with the Southerners and with President Buchanan.

The Lincoln-Douglas Debates have, nevertheless, become the subject of legend:

There was, however, in all [Lincoln] said, a tone of earnest truthfulness of elevated, noble sentiment, and of kindly sympathy . . .
Carl Schurz, a contemporary supporter, quoted in Angle (ed.), *The Lincoln Reader*, Greenwood Press, 1947.

Lincoln's nobility, his candour, his inspired foresight, have been contrasted with

---

1860 was the year of the next Presidential election. Was Lincoln throwing away the Senate to gain the Presidency? Was he being ambitious for his party or for himself? He went on to say that it was the principle at stake that mattered, not his personal victory in the contest for the Senate.

This should knock on the head any sentimental myths about Lincoln's views. (Even free states such as Illinois could and did have laws against racially mixed marriages.)

Douglas had opposed the pro-slavery Lecompton Constitution for Kansas on the grounds that it was the product of bogus elections and therefore was not consistent with popular sovereignty (Lincoln was not convinced that Douglas could be trusted in this matter.)

William H. Seward. More prominent than Lincoln, he held broadly the same views on slavery but ended up as President Lincoln's Secretary of State.

Brogan is outlining the legend. He did not actually support it.

Douglas's low cunning, shameless evasion, downright dishonesty . . .
Brogan, *Abraham Lincoln.*

However, the truth seems to be that both men resorted to a certain amount of distortion, and Douglas's position was *not* devoid of principle in America as it then was:

We ought to extend to the negro race . . . all the rights, all the privileges, and the immunities which they can exercise consistently with the safety of society . . . The question then arises, what are those privileges, and what is the nature and extent of them? My answer is, that that is a question which each state must answer for

This was in itself a fairly moderate position, typical of many Northern Democrats. But Southern Democrats were not prepared to be so liberal.

itself . . .
Douglas at Alton, Illinois, 15 October 1858; quoted in Blum, Morgan *et al.*, *The National Experience*, Part I, Harcourt Brace Jovanovich Inc., New York, 1963.

On the whole, any attempt to add luster to Lincoln's fame by belittling Douglas or by exaggerating the seriousness of differences between the two men, would be a perversion of history.
James G. Randall, *Lincoln the President*, Vol. I, quoted in Angle, *The Lincoln Reader.*

It seems that in reality both men spoke persuasively in the view of those who were not strongly partisan:

I felt so sorry for Lincoln while Douglas was speaking, and then to my surprise I felt *so* sorry for Douglas when Lincoln replied.
Mrs William Crotty of Seneca, Illinois, quoted in Tarbell, *The Life of Abraham Lincoln*, Vol. I.

In the last analysis, the principles of both Lincoln and Douglas would have closed Kansas to slavery if honestly applied. To twentieth-century eyes Lincoln's principles may look more morally acceptable, but at the time Douglas's position probably made more practical sense.

* * *

If the principled arguments of Lincoln had been heard and taken note of in the East he was still a long way from federal office. He had demonstrated that, in Douglas's words, he was, 'the strong man of the party – full of wit, facts, dates – and the best stump speaker . . . in the West.' However, the leading figure in the Republican Party, and the most likely Republican candidate for the Presidency in 1860 was still an Easterner, William Seward.

The 1860 Electoral Campaign

The years 1858 to 1861 were the most extraordinary in Lincoln's life. Against a background of ever-mounting tension over the slavery issue, he won the Republican Party nomination, was elected President of the United States, and then found himself Commander in Chief of the Union in a civil war with the breakaway Southern states. Yet he was completely untested; with the exception of his short period in the House of Representatives, he had no experience of Washington, and he had no experience at all of executive government.

Lincoln's official biographers, Nicolay and Hay, portrayed his rise to the White House as heroic and almost inevitable. This picture was enduring:

Men felt a sudden reverence for a mind and heart developed to these noble proportions . . . They turned instinctively to one so familiar with strife for help in solving the desperate problem with which the nation grappled.
Tarbell, *The Life of Abraham Lincoln*, Vol. I.

The legend-building which has gone on around Lincoln's rise to the Presidency has been added to by his own caution and modesty:

1858
. . . there is no such good luck in store for me as the Presidency of these United States.

April 1859
I must in all candour say I do not think myself fit for the Presidency.

July 1859
I have enlisted for the permanent success of the Republican cause, and for this object I shall labor faithfully in the ranks . . . .
Quoted in Tarbell, *The Life of Abraham Lincoln*, Vol. I.

The ritual in American politics of prospective candidates denying that they are going to seek nomination has a long pedigree! Lincoln's guarded comments were probably genuine, but he *did* have ambition. Opponents thought his modesty was a front. Democrats had already referred to his 'snivelling humility'.

Undoubtedly, Lincoln's strengths of character played an important part in securing him the Presidency, but the story is also one of luck, political manipulation and the peculiarities of the American electoral system.

Though by no means unknown, Lincoln was far from being the obvious Republican choice.
Maldwyn A. Jones *The Limits of Liberty*, O.U.P., 1983.

Winning the Republican nomination

In early 1859, Lincoln's long and uncomfortable years on the Illinois Court Circuit began to pay off. Judge David Davis, Judge Logan and Leonard Swett, together with shrewd politicians such as John M. Palmer, began to sow the seeds of the idea that Illinois should nominate Lincoln as the Republican candidate for 1860. Lincoln was carefully 'talked up' in newspaper offices and in political society. By the end of 1859, although Lincoln still denied it, it was a real possibility that the Illinois party would put forward his name, so much so that Lincoln was persuaded to write a short 'autobiography' for campaigning purposes.

He was reluctant to do so, perhaps for reasons of modesty, but also because he was ashamed of his humble origins, even though they were to become a major electoral asset.

Other careful political preparations were also afoot. The journalist Joseph Medill was canvassing support for Lincoln amongst Congressmen in Washington. Then, in early 1860, Norman B. Judd persuaded the Republican National Committee to hold the National Convention (at which the Republican candidate would be chosen) in Chicago. This was a remarkable decision. Chicago was a ramshackle, half-built boom town, and never before had a National Convention been held so far west, but for the Lincoln supporters it was like being told that they would be playing the vital cup-tie on their home ground.

The Illinois State Convention was held at Decatur on 9 and 10 May. Lincoln was adopted overwhelmingly, following a remarkable demonstration which was to set the tone of the rest of the campaign. A banner, stretched between two weather-beaten fence rails, was paraded into the convention hall. It read:

ABRAHAM LINCOLN
THE RAIL CANDIDATE
FOR PRESIDENT IN 1860

Two rails from a lot of 3000 made in 1830 by Thos. Hanks and Abe Lincoln – whose father was the first pioneer of Macon County

Whether or not the rails were genuine is unclear, but they became the symbol of his candidacy.
Lincoln hated being known as 'Abe', including the appellation 'Honest Abe', and also winced at incorrect spellings such as 'Abram'. (The banner should have read *John* Hanks.)

Thus the humble pioneer pedigree of the substantial lawyer from Springfield was established. This was of vital importance, because the waves of European immigration to the United States, and the western movement, had steadily shifted the electoral centre of gravity in the nation away from the settled and 'civilized' society of the East Coast.

From the late eighteenth century onwards the frontier of white settlement moved progressively westward beyond the Appalachian mountains. According to the statistical abstract of the United States, the centre of population of the United States was 23 miles east of Baltimore in 1790, 23 miles south-east of Parkersburg, West Virginia, in 1850, and six miles south-east of Columbus, Indiana, by 1900.

However, the East was still important, and on the whole it was committed to Seward, even though prominent Eastern Republicans such as Horace Greeley were quietly working to undermine the front-runner. As late as May 1860, Lincoln seems to have gone largely unmentioned in the Republican journals of the East, but his name had very definitely been heard, and he had been very active on his own behalf. In 1859 Lincoln had collected and published his 1858 speeches, and since then he had undertaken speaking tours such as that to Ohio in 1859. Then, in February and March of 1860, he raised his banner in the territory of his main rival by speaking in the North-Eastern states. Introduced optimistically at Manchester as the next President of the United States, he made his most important appearance on this tour at the Cooper Institute in New York. To the accompaniment of a snow storm raging outside he gave an impassioned but carefully reasoned speech, insisting that although the Republicans would not interfere with slavery where it already existed, they could not accept its extension. Lincoln ended:

> Let us have faith that right makes might, and in that faith, *let us*, to the end, dare to do our duty as we understand it.
> Quoted in Oates, *With Malice Towards None.*

At the Cooper Institute Lincoln was given a standing ovation. By the end of his tour there were influential Easterners who thought that Lincoln might give Seward a run for his money.

The Republican Convention of 1860 opened in Chicago on 16 May. Built on the marshy shore of Lake Michigan, half the buildings and sidewalks of Chicago lay on a level with the mud and the rest were in the process of being raised on stilts. Chicago was literally building itself up, and hosting the Convention was part of the process. The town was besieged with visitors and delegates. In an atmosphere of growing and almost feverish excitement, the streets rang to the sounds of both spontaneous and carefully organized demonstrations for the various nominees.

Yet Lincoln was still the outsider. Seward had 150 Convention delegates who were committed to support him – 83 short of the number he needed for victory. The other contenders were Chase of Ohio, Bates from Missouri, and Cameron from Pennsylvania. Each of these had around 50 delegates. Lincoln had 22.

Lincoln's eventual triumph no doubt came as a surprise to many at the time, but we can see with the benefit of hindsight that he was a stronger contender than at first appears. The Republicans had to choose a candidate who would attract support from as many parts of the United States as possible (although it was never likely that the Party would win any significant support in the South). But Chase had a reputation as a radical and did not even possess the full support of the Ohio delegation. Bates was a former slave owner and member of the American Party (a Party hostile to European immigrants); as such he was objectionable to the significant German populations in Illinois and Wisconsin. Cameron was a former Democrat lacking in clear principles and suspected by some of having amassed a private fortune in public office. By comparison, Lincoln had the advantage of a relatively clean sheet, having only recently emerged into national politics, together with the reputation born of the Lincoln-Douglas Debates. There was a real chance that Lincoln could pick up support form the Chase, Bates and Cameron delegates on the grounds that there were fewer objections to Lincoln and he might win a wider spread of support in the elections.

Lincoln still had to beat Seward. But there were objections to Seward as well. He was accused of Whiggish arrogance by former Democrats, and there were suspicions that he had been involved in unscrupulous political dealings with his ally, 'Boss' Weed, from New York. Worst of all, Seward was suspected of being a radical, with liberal Republican sympathies. Although this radical image was undeserved, Seward had spoken of the 'irrepressible conflict' with slavery, and supporters of slavery blamed Seward's rhetoric for the recent attempted armed insurrection by the abolitionist John Brown. All of this made Seward unlikely to pick up votes in the lower North (the areas bordering the slave states) and this cast doubt on his ability to win a Presidential election. By comparison, Lincoln's carefully judged public pronouncements on slavery made him more acceptable in the lower North, even though his *policy* was effectively the same as Seward's.

I.e. that he was in favour of the abolition of slavery.

See p. 43.

What Lincoln needed was a shrewd political manager who could persuade the delegates at Chicago to switch their votes in Lincoln's direction. Lincoln had such a man in Judge David Davis. Davis set out to lobby and cajole delegates; he and his team worked almost ceaselessly round the clock in the run-up to the balloting on 18 May. But it was not just reason and argument that swayed men's minds. Offers of jobs in a future Lincoln administration had to be made too, as Dr Ray, one of Davis's team, telegraphed to Lincoln, who did not attend the Convention: 'A pledge or two may be necessary when the pinch comes.' Even so, Lincoln probably remained in touch with his basic integrity; he telegraphed to Davis: 'Make no contracts that will bind me.'

The voting was carried out in the Wigwam, a purpose-built hall with a semi-circular roof, capable of holding 10,000 people. The building was packed with wildly excited supporters, and Davis had made sure that Lincoln had the loudest.

At the announcement of Lincoln's name there was such a noise that according to one observer 'a thousand steam whistles, ten acres of hotel gongs, a tribe of Comanches [sic], headed by a choice vanguard from pandemonium, might have mingled in the scene unnoticed'.

The first vote gave Seward 173½, Lincoln 102, and the rest came virtually nowhere. Lincoln, in touch by telegraph and apparently geared up to face yet another failure in his political career, was amazed. On the second ballot Lincoln's vote rose to 181 as the delegates switched votes away from the back-runners. Then, on the third ballot, Lincoln topped the 234 votes necessary for an overall majority. He was the Republican Party candidate for the Presidency. Hannibal Hamlin would run with him for the Vice Presidency.

Why had Lincoln won the nomination?

> The system of election comprised a series of votes, with delegates changing their allegiances between votes, until one candidate had an overall majority (i.e. more than 50% of the votes cast).

. . . he had already demonstrated that he was a match for the likely Democratic choice, Douglas. His birth in a log cabin and his ability to split rails made it possible to present him as a man of the people. Finally his managers, led by Judge David Davis of Chicago, astutely packed the convention hall with noisy Lincoln supporters, and, more important, secured the support of key delegations by the promise – or half promise – of Cabinet posts.
Jones, *The Limits of Liberty*.

Donald has a blunter verdict:

. . . by 1860 he had manoeuvred himself into a position where he controlled the party machinery, platform and candidates of one of the pivotal states of the Union.
Donald, *Lincoln Reconsidered*.

Lincoln was far removed from being guileless and unsophisticated!

Winning the Presidency

Lincoln's candidacy was greeted with delight in the North-West; bonfires of tar-barrels and fence posts blazed across Illinois. In the East, Republicans were more enthusiastic for their party than for their candidate, about whom they still knew relatively little. But when the Eastern Democrats attacked Lincoln, calling him a 'third-rate country lawyer', a teller of 'coarse and clumsy jokes' and jeering at the label 'honest old Abe', the *New York Tribune* retaliated:

A man who by his own genius and force of character has raised himself from being

Marching music for the Presidential campaign. 'Wigwam' refers to the building in Chicago in which the Republican Convention was held. Published in Boston, it was important to get the candidate's face known 'back east'.

This is the usual image of Lincoln, and is in its way valid, but what lingering doubts might Republicans have had?

See pp. 33-34.

a penniless and uneducated flat boatman on the Wabash River to the position Mr Lincoln now occupies is not likely to be a nullity anywhere.
Quoted in Tarbell, *The Life of Abraham Lincoln*, Vol. I.

Seward and the other defeated candidates for the Republican nomination rallied behind Lincoln, and the party bandwagon began to roll: the 'rail-splitter' image became a positive electoral asset.

The Republicans were confident that they would win the election of 1860. They had come a strong second to the Democrats in 1856, but now the Democrats were split right down the middle. The Democrats had held their Convention in Charleston, South Carolina, in April 1860. Many people expected that Douglas would be adopted as their candidate, and he was the favourite of the Northern Democrats. However, his rejection of the Lecompton Constitution and his authorship of the Freeport Doctrine had

Buchanan had decided not to stand for re-election. His Presidency had seen both party and nation split.

greatly upset Southern Democrats. The Southern Democrats wanted the party platform for the forthcoming election to include federal protection of slavery in the territories and laws for the protection of slave property throughout the Union. The Northern Democrats simply could not accept these demands. The Charleston Convention broke up and was reconvened at Baltimore in June. But again agreement could not be reached. The Convention split. The Northern Democrats nominated Douglas to run on a platform of popular sovereignty. The Southern Democrats nominated John C. Breckinridge of Kentucky. Following the Democratic split Lincoln wrote: '. . . it really appears now, as if the success of the Republican ticket is inevitable.'

The election was turned into a four-way contest by the emergence of the Constitutional Party. This was a party of former Whigs from the border states who hoped to head off the growing sectional conflict between the North and the South. Their candidate for the Presidency was John Bell of Tennessee, and Edward Everett of Massachusetts was his running mate.

The Republican Party platform for the election was clear and positive. Slavery should be contained within those states where it already existed and not allowed in the territories. However, the party reaffirmed that it had no intention of interfering with slavery where it already existed. But the Republicans were not a 'one-idea' party; their platform included legislation to assist the establishemnt of homesteads, the increase of tariffs, and the construction as soon as possible of a transcontinental railroad.

These policies were designed to encourage settlement in the West and the growth of industry.

The Republicans campaigned with great enthusiasm. Rallies and meetings were addressed by leading party orators speaking from platforms adorned with banners, the elephant symbol of the Republicans, the rail fence symbol of Lincoln and the Stars and Stripes. There were torchlight parades by young Republican supporters, who were known as Wide-Awakes. The newspapers were filled with savage invective from all parties. But although Douglas (for the first time in a Presidential contest) stumped the Union, Lincoln remained aloof in Springfield. From his doorway he waved to visitors, and he conferred with and wrote to his party managers, but he refused to make any public pronouncements. This was partly because he wanted to unite his party around its agreed platform and partly because he did not wish to give any opportunities to his opponents. It may also have been that he believed he should quietly await the verdict of the nation with genuine humility.

Election day was 6 November. Lincoln awaited the results sprawled on a sofa in the telegraph office at Springfield. By the small hours of the following morning he knew that he had been elected President of the United States, although it took another 24 hours for all the results to come in.

After years of disappointment and at the age of 51 he had achieved not just a public office, but the highest public office in the land. He did so in the midst of the most serious internal crisis that the United States has ever faced, for she was in imminent danger of splitting apart. The voting figures in the 1860 Presidential election make this clear.

Each state is entitled to vote for a number of Presidential electors, who, in their turn, vote in the electoral college and actually choose the President. The number of Presidential electors per state is proportional to its population. Broadly speaking, if a candidate wins the popular vote in a particular state then he collects the electoral votes of that state although sometimes the electoral vote may split. It is a system which has, from time to time, had odd results.

Lincoln took 40% of the popular vote (1,866,452) and collected 180 votes in the electoral college. This gave him a clear majority of electoral votes over all the other candidates combined, but Douglas, who came second in the popular vote with 1,376,957, only came fourth in the electoral college, with 12 electoral votes. This was because Lincoln's support was concentrated in the populous Northern free states, California and Oregon, and he received all of their electoral votes with the exception of New Jersey, which split. Douglas's popular support was also high, but it was spread too widely for him to pick up many electoral votes. By comparison

Breckinridge picked up 72 electoral votes from a popular vote of only 849,781, concentrated in the less populous Southern slave-owning states.

Thus, although Lincoln had won fair and square, there were some very worrying features of the election. Lincoln had more popular votes than any other single candidate, but together, the other candidates had nearly a million votes more than him. More importantly, 15 states had given him no electoral votes, and in ten states he had received not a single popular vote. Lincoln, the man who has gone down in history as the saviour of the unity of the United States, was in fact elected by the Northern, non-slave section of the republic and by a minority of the popular vote; his party was clearly a *sectional* party. Thus although Oates says 'nobody could label [Lincoln] an "accidental" President . . .' it is also true that, ironically, it was actually Douglas and not Lincoln who was, the only 'national' candidate in the field.

Lincoln's election confirmed Southerners in their belief that they would now be ruled by the Northerners and that it was only a matter of time before a majority of Northerners in Congress would start to pass legislation hostile to the 'peculiar institution' of the South.

I.e. slavery.

Lincoln was now in a difficult position. He was President Elect, but would not take up office until March 1861. In the meantime, the Union was falling apart. The Southern States were already in the process of seceding. Lincoln was powerless to do anything about it, for President Buchanan, a Democrat, was still the head of government.

The path to secession

The election in 1860 of a President committed to preventing the extension of slavery in the territories brought to a peak tension between the North and South over the slavery issue.

Following the Lincoln-Douglas Debates in 1858 it had become less and less likely that the Southern slave owners would accept Douglas's doctrine of popular sovereignty for the territories. A growing number of Southerners wanted Congress to enact 'black codes', which would impose slavery on the Western settlers. Southerners believed that slavery was the basis of their entire way of life and that the homesteaders, traders, bankers and industrialists of the North were intent on destroying the identity of the

Harriet Tubman (extreme left), with a group of slaves whom she helped to escape. The Fugitive Slave Law said that runaways such as these could be taken back whence they had come, but it cost federal authorities $40,000 and 1000 soldiers to get Anthony Burns back to Virginia from Massachusetts in 1854. The Fugitive Slave Law was not enforced in Massachusetts after this.

South. Therefore the Southerners wanted positive action to protect their institutions. Unless slavery was allowed to spread, the slave owners would eventually be out-voted by the opponents of slavery in Congress.

Tempers rose higher over the fugitive slave laws. Under the Fugitive Slave Act of 1850 a runaway slave fleeing to a free state could be captured and returned to his master. This happened in 1854, in the case of Anthony Burns, but only in the face of massive Northern opposition and at huge expense. Following this, free states started to pass 'personal liberty laws', which punished citizens who helped federal officers to enforce the Fugitive Slave Act. When a man called Booth rescued a runaway slave in Wisconsin the federal courts held that he had committed an offence against the 1850 Act, but the Wisconsin State Supreme Court declared that the 1850 Act was unconstitutional. The upshot of the dispute was that Booth ended up back in a federal jail, but the problem had not been resolved.

I.e. 'John Brown's Body'.

The Burns and Booth cases were followed in October 1859 by an event which provoked great anger in the South. The radical anti-slavery leader John Brown had formulated a wild scheme to establish a militant abolitionist movement, and he captured the Federal Armoury at Harper's Ferry, Virginia. Although Brown ended on the gallows, thereby giving the abolitionists both a martyr and a song, the Southerners were terrified by what they justifiably regarded as Brown's attempt to incite a slave revolt. Southerners chose to ignore the fact that most Northerners and Republicans also condemned Brown's action; instead, the Southerners believed that it was only a foretaste of what the abolitionists might be planning.

Thus, by the time of the Democratic Party Convention at Charleston in April 1860, Southerners – as we have already seen – were demanding Congressional action to establish slavery in the territories, and the destruction of the 'personal liberty laws'. Some Southern Democrats went further: Yancey of Alabama demanded that the Democrats should affirm that slavery was *right*, and was already talking about seceding from the Union in the event of a Republican victory in the Presidential election.

By this time, the Southerners believed that the Republicans were a sectional party which represented Northern interests and was intent upon the abolition of slavery. Consequently, Lincoln's victory in the Presidential

John Brown kisses a black baby before being hanged for his anti-slavery rebellion at Harper's Ferry, Virginia. Were his actions justified, or was he merely a nineteenth-century terrorist?

election of November 1860 turned talk of secession into reality. On 20 December the State Legislature of South Carolina, meeting in Charleston, declared: '. . . the Union now subsisting between South Carolina and other States under the name of "The United States of America" is hereby dissolved.' By February 1861 seven Southern states had seceded from the Union. On 4 February their representatives met in Montgomery, Alabama, and on 8 February they established the Confederate States of America.

From secession to civil war

Put simply, Lincoln believed that the Confederate States had no right to secede:

Lincoln went on to develop the argument that the Constitution was a contract freely entered into, and binding on all parties.

I hold that, in contemplation of universal law and of the Constitution, the Union of these States is perpetual.
Extract from Lincoln's First Inaugural Address; quoted in Commager, *Documents of American History*.

Nevertheless, in the four months between his election and his inauguration there was little that Lincoln could do about the secessionist states. He remained optimistic, firstly because he thought that secession was a folly which the Southerners would eventually recognize, and secondly because he thought that support for the Union was still strong in the South:

What political motive might Lincoln have had for writing this?

The people of the South have too much of good sense and good temper to attempt the ruin of the government . . .
Lincoln, August 1860.

See pp. 11-13.

Lincoln may have been correct in viewing secession as a folly, but the secessionist argument had strong roots in the theory of states' rights. Secession was a folly with which the Southerners were determined to continue, especially when they remembered that behind the official lines of Republican policy lurked the hope expressed by both Lincoln and Seward

THE RAIL CANDIDATE.

Being the 'Rail Candidate' was not necessarily an easy ride – Lincoln literally sitting on the fence (Greeley, editor of the New York Tribune, *later criticised Lincoln's failure to free the slaves).*

that slavery could be set on the path towards eventual extinction. Consequently, Lincoln's second belief – in Unionism among the Southerners – was clearly wrong.

As President Elect he erred badly in dismissing the secessionist crisis as 'an artificial one' and in exaggerating the strength of Southern Unionism.
Jones, *The Limits of Liberty.*

Being a party of the Northern section, the Republicans actually had little real knowledge of the state of public opinion in the South.

However, Lincoln was not the only Republican to make this mistake; many other Republican leaders saw Southerners' threats to secede if Lincoln were elected as a political bluff.

While the President Elect sat on the side-lines, the retiring President clearly refused to take any decisive action over secession. Lincoln's view was that it was constitutionally within the President's powers to use force to continue the collection of federal taxes in the South, and it became Lincoln's policy that he would maintain the presence of federal authority in the South and wait for secessionism to collapse. But there was little direct action that he could take.

The period up to March 1861 did not lack attempts at compromise. John C. Crittenden of Kentucky proposed that the Missouri Compromise line of 36° 30′ North should be re-established and continued clear across the continent to the Pacific; slavery would be recognized south of that line, even protected by federal laws, but not north of it. However, the Crittenden proposals had a sting in the tail: amendments to the consitution would effectively guarantee slavery for ever where it already existed. The Republicans rejected the Crittenden plan; they did not want to return to the Missouri Compromise and refused to budge from the principle of 'no extension of slavery'. Lincoln remained publicly silent on the Crittenden compromise, despite growing criticism of him, but in private he urged:

Why should Lincoln remain quiet in public? Might he compromise on issues other than the extension of slavery?

Entertain no compromise in regard to the *extension* of slavery. The instant you do, they have us under again; . . . The tug has come, and better now than later.
Quoted in Blum, Morgan et. al. *The National Experience*, Part I.

Lincoln's reluctance to compromise at this point has led some historians to say that in one sense the ensuing civil war was Lincoln's fault:

As far as any one man was responsible for a decision which might involve war, it was Lincoln.
Brogan, *Abraham Lincoln.*

See p. 56 and compare with p. 59.

In a narrow sense this was true, but perhaps it is not entirely fair. There were other attempts at compromise which *also* failed, and even as late as Lincoln's inauguration (4 March 1861) he was stating that he did not intend to abolish slavery where it already existed, and that he did not have the constitutional authority to do so. Lincoln was still trying to explain himself and keep bridges intact. But Southerners refused to believe that what Lincoln said was a guarantee for slavery. In a sense, the Southerners were right. If slavery were banned in the territories and in new states entering the Union, then eventually there would be enough free states to amend the Constitution and abolish slavery completely.

An amendment to the Constitution requires a two-thirds majority of Congress.

Lincoln himself now appeared to be delaying the process of dealing with the secessionist states. First, there had been the matter of physically getting to Washington. This had been achieved by means of a triumphant railroad tour. At each stop Lincoln blandly assured the crowds that there was nothing wrong with the Union; but the journey was not without danger,

This railroad tour was more or less followed in reverse by the funeral train in 1865.

Lincoln's first inauguration. He had recently grown the beard to hide his scrawny neck. Chief Justice Roger B. Taney sits behind, not looking very amused as Lincoln makes a firm but conciliatary speech outside Congress.

and an alleged assassination plot in Baltimore required the services of the Pinkerton Detective Agency and a secret early morning arrival in the capital. Lincoln was feeling the stress of the situation; what we would nowadays call a psychic experience led him to believe that he would never return home from Washington alive.

Then he had to spend time appointing his Cabinet, a complicated and unpleasant process in which he had to pay off political debts and balance the factions in his party. Seward became Secretary of State, Chase became Secretary of the Treasury, and Cameron became Secretary of War, an unsatisfactory appointment which was changed in 1862 when Stanton took over.

. . . to the Whitehouse (although still called, variously, the Executive Mansion, or the President's House). Lincoln was ashamed of his log-cabin origins, but not of this.

Fort Sumter, during its 36-hour bombardment by the Confederates.

Seward had engaged in secret negotiations with the South and may have believed he could 'run' Lincoln. Lincoln confronted Seward in private.

But even when Lincoln had arrived in Washington, had sorted out the problem of Cabinet appointments and had been inaugurated, he still held back from decisive action. William Seward and other Republicans felt confirmed in the view that Lincoln lacked the power to command, and Seward was busy hatching some wild, unstatesmanlike plans of his own. Lincoln had to put Seward in his place, and Seward was forced to acknowledge Lincoln's ability: 'Executive force and vigor are rare qualities . . . The President is the best of us'.

In *A Concise History of the American Republic* (1977) Morison, Commager and Leuchtenburg offered the explanation that 'Lincoln delayed decision, not from fear, but because he was watching Virginia [which was in the process of deciding whether or not to secede].' Lincoln thought that by avoiding sudden action the crucial state of Virginia (a slave state) might remain in the Union. But as hopes of this evaporated, Lincoln decided at the end of March that it was time to act. He resolved to send reinforcements to the federal garrison at Fort Sumter, an island fortress in the middle of Charleston harbour, South Carolina, under siege from Confederate forces.

Sumter had become a symbol of federal authority – it had no strategic value. The relief expedition was fatally weakened by Seward's meddling, but even before it arrived Jefferson Davis ordered General P.G.T. Beaureguard to bombard Sumter into submission. Fire was opened in the early morning of 12 April 1861. The relief expedition turned up later in the day but was unable to get through. Pounded by artillery, Fort Sumter surrendered honourably and without loss of life on 14 April. Lincoln's policy had now become clear: he would not agree to the secession of the South and had, therefore, sent the relief expedition to Fort Sumter; but if there had to be fighting it was the Southerners who had fired the first shots. Lincoln declared that the Southerners were in rebellion against the legal authority of the United States. Congress agreed, and so, apparently, did the Northern states. A wave of patriotic fervour swept the North, and when Lincoln issued a proclamation calling for 75,000 militia, the War Department very soon found itself struggling to deal with over 91,000 volunteers. War had begun.

Lincoln and the Civil War

The American Civil War, which lasted from 1861 to 1865, was perhaps the first 'modern' war. It was fought by huge armies, part volunteer, part conscript, across a theatre of operations which stretched from the East

New technology adapted for war. The American Civil War was the first conflict in which railways played a really major part. This weapon is a siege mortar.

Attrition: the strategy of wearing away the enemy, even at the cost of great losses to your own side, in the belief that your enemy will be exhausted first.

Coast to the Mississippi. It was the first war (with the exception of the Crimea) in which railroads played a significant part, and the first war in which the brutality of attrition was eventually accepted as a necessary strategy. For the first time the fruits of the Industrial Revolution and of evolving technology were harnessed for the purposes of destruction, although they appeared side by side with the cavalry charge, the dispatch rider, and perhaps the last flowering of old-fashioned military chivalry. It was also the first war conducted under the leadership of elected heads of government, for apparently high ideals. By the time the North had won the war, over 600,000 men had been killed; that was the cost of preventing the Southern states from leaving the Union, and of abolishing slavery.

The fighting

With the benefit of hindsight the victory of the North looks like a foregone conclusion. The Northern population was more than three times the white population of the South. The North had four-fifths of the nation's manufacturing industry and the greater share of all other forms of wealth. The material superiority of the North was bound to triumph in the end. The Northern General William T. Sherman said 'in all history no nation of mere agriculturalists ever made a successful war against mechanics.'

The top stratum of Southern society consisted of a class of great landowners, believed to be skilled in outdoor pursuits such as riding and shooting.

However, at the start of the war the outcome did not seem so predictable. Many commentators thought that the supposedly superior military qualities of the 'aristocratic' Southerners would triumph in a short and decisive struggle. The Southerners were fighting to protect the 'independence' of their homelands and could be expected to show greater fighting spirit. The strategic nature of the war favoured the South as well: the Southerners had simply to remain independent in order to win, whereas the Northerners had the far greater task of conquering and occupying the South. Above all, many observers thought that the Southern Confederacy had the better and more experienced leader in the shape of President Jefferson Davis. By comparison, Lincoln was an unknown quantity, well versed in the arts of frontier politics, but completely untried in administration. Wendell Phillips had described Lincoln as: 'a huckster in politics . . . a first rate second rate man.'

Wendell Phillips was an abolitionist from Boston who was highly critical of Lincoln because of his moderation.

Huckster: A trader or mercenary.

As it turned out, the South was not able to win a quick victory, and Lincoln proved to be the more effective leader. But it took time to mobilize the crushing power of the North, and mistakes were made along the way. The longer the war went on, the more likely it was that the North would

Major campaigns of the American Civil War.

Scott's plan was named after the giant Anaconda snake of South America which kills its prey by constriction.

win, but, paradoxically, it still took four years of bitter fighting to gain a result.

The Confederates seemed to have the upper hand during the first two years of the war. By comparison, the Northerners appeared stumbling and uncertain. The commander of the Union army was the ageing Winfield Scott, hero of the Mexican War. His plan was to encircle and constrict the South. But Lincoln was under considerable public pressure to pull off a quick victory (as always, everybody thought that the war ought to be over by Christmas). Scott's plan was rapidly abandoned, with the exception of a crucial naval blockade, in favour of an attempt by General Irwin McDowell to strike directly at the Confederate capital of Richmond, Virginia.

However, McDowell was defeated at the First Battle of Bull Run in July 1861. This was a clash between two almost equally unprepared armies,

Greeley, like other 'supporters', often did not give Lincoln much help!

A FAMILY QUARREL.

From Punch *28 September 1861. Lincoln, just about recognizable in federal costume, confronts a person who is probably supposed to be Jefferson Davis (complete with Confederate apron) but who succeeds in looking remarkably like Mrs Lincoln. Is the relevance of this to the Lincoln's own domestic situation accidental?*

obstructed by sightseers, and it left Washington completely open to capture; Lincoln's Presidential career very nearly finished almost as soon as it started! Lincoln was criticized from all directions and defeatism hung in the air. Horace Greeley, editor of the *New York Tribune*, wrote to him: 'You are not considered a great man.'

Keeping his nerve, Lincoln appointed the dashing young George B. McClellan to train up the volunteer recruits into the efficient Army of the Potomac. McClellan was more cautious in practice than his flamboyant personality suggested. When he eventually brought his men into action on the peninsula between the James and York rivers, in a controversial attempt to capture Richmond from that direction, he became bogged down. His adversary in the Peninsular Campaign was the brilliant Confederate general Robert E. Lee. After the Seven Days' Battle, McClellan was pulled back, and command given to Halleck.

In August 1862, Union forces again found themselves driven back to Washington in the Second Battle of Bull Run, following which McClellan returned to favour. Faced with the problem of countering Lee's thrust to the west of Washington, McClellan gave battle at Antietam, in September 1862. On the single most bloody day of the war, a lucky stalemate was achieved, but McClellan had failed to deliver the final decisive attack and Lincoln decided that he could no longer tolerate generals who suffered from 'the slows'. McClellan's replacement was the rash Ambrose Burnside, of whom Lincoln said that he was the only man who could snatch defeat from the jaws of victory. After a foolhardy attack on entrenched Confederate positions at Fredericksburg, Virginia, in December 1862, Burnside was replaced by 'Fighting' Joe Hooker.

Thus in the East the Union war effort had been marked largely by defeat and a confusing succession of changes in command. Only in the West did the Union seem to be making any headway. The tough and hard-drinking young Ulysses S. Grant had occupied Kentucky and then split the Confederate forces in Tennessee by taking a flotilla of gunboats up the Tennessee river. Then at Shiloh (April 1862) Grant narrowly defeated the Confederates and drove them back to Corinth, where his commanding officer, Halleck, finished off the job and gained most of the credit. Meanwhile, David Farragut of the Union navy had seized the lower end of the Mississippi, giving the Union control of the entire length of the Mississippi valley, with the exception of the section between Vicksburg and Port Hudson.

General W.T. Sherman on campaign and looking relentless.

Ulysses Grant outside his tent, June 1864, looking more like the storekeeper that he had once been than a great general and future President of the United States.

Grant (left), better dressed than contemporary accounts would have you believe receives Lee's surrender at Appomatox Court House. It was a quiet and dignified affair; neither of them seems very happy, but after the slaughter of their recent campaigns there was not much to be joyful about.

1863 was the turning point of the war. In the east, 'Fighting' Joe Hooker did not live up to his name and was replaced by George G. Meade, 'Old Snapping Turtle'. When Lee attempted an invasion of the North via the Shenandoah Valley, Meade met him at Gettysburg, Pennsylvania (July 1863). Gettysburg was a grinding, defensive battle of attrition which produced 50,000 casualties over three days; it gave a clear hint of what modern war was going to become. Lee's army of North Virginia was destroyed as an offensive force and withdrew southwards, spending the next two years making its final defeat as costly as possible.

Simultaneously with the battle of Gettysburg, the Confederate stronghold of Vicksburg on the Mississippi fell to Grant's remorseless siege tactics. The entire Mississippi was now in Union hands. By the end of 1863 Grant had been given supreme command in the West, and bitter fighting around Chatenooga in south-east Tennessee placed him in a position to invade Georgia and split the Confederacy in two.

The events of 1863 had solved Lincoln's command problem. Grant was now created Lieutenant General in command of all land forces and transferred to the East, leaving the forces at Chatenooga in the hands of the equally determined William Tecumseh Sherman. Lincoln, Grant and Sherman now evolved a new kind of war, in which the greater strength and resources of the North were used to grind down the South. Men were judged to be expendable; prisoners of war were no longer exchanged, with terrible results. Grant had done the arithmetic and knew that the South would collapse before the North did. Grant concluded:

> The art of war is simple enough. Find out where your enemy is. Get at him as soon as you can. Strike him as hard as you can, and keep moving on.
> Quoted in Donald, *Lincoln Reconsidered*.

Lincoln accepted the implications of Grant's approach, even though he had always hoped that the war was one which 'had peace in its belly'.

By July 1864, Sherman reached Atlanta in Georgia and then burned and destroyed his way to the sea at Savannah, wrecking the Southern economy as he went. He then turned north through South and North Carolina, and in early 1865 was heading for Richmond, Virginia.

In Virginia, Grant followed a policy of attrition against Lee. Three great battles in 1864 – the Wilderness, Spotsylvania Court House and Cold Harbour – inflicted terrible casualties on both sides. Lee's military brilliance was undimmed, but Grant's troops kept on coming. The final bitter fighting took place around Petersburg, Richmond's railroad link to

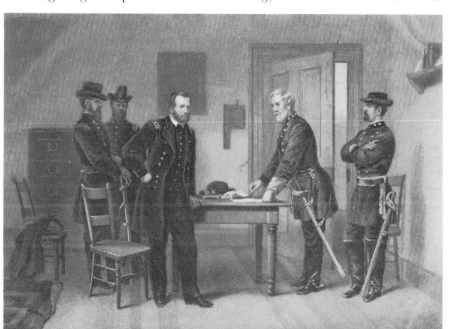

the South. When Petersburg fell, in April 1865, the war was effectively over. Union forces entered the ruins of Richmond. The final pursuit of Lee's forces ended at Appomatox Court House on 9 April. In a courteous ceremony, Lee surrendered to Grant, who was dressed in a private's uniform. The North had won.

Lincoln the war leader

As President, Lincoln was Commander in Chief, but of course he was also in charge of the administrative, diplomatic and political conduct of the war. In a very simple sense, therefore, the victory was his, and he was the hero of the nation:

Emerson was a philosopher, poet and essayist, born in Massachusetts and active in the anti-slavery movement. Why should the date of this make you cautious?

> In four years – four years of battle-days – his endurance, his fertility of resources, his magnanimity, were sorely tried and never found wanting. There, by his courage, his justice, his even temper, his fertile counsel, his humanity, he stood a heroic figure in the centre of a heroic epoch. He is the true history of the American people in his time.
> Ralph Waldo Emerson, 1865.

However, during the war itself Lincoln had come under a constant barrage of criticism and pressure from almost all shades of opinion in the North. What is more, it is only in retrospect that Lincoln's policies were justified by eventual victory:

Donald is not saying that Lincoln *was* a failure, but *is* saying something important about the way we look at History.

> . . . had the President been defeated in [the Presidential election of] 1864 he would have been written off as one of the great failures of the American political system – the man who let his country drift into civil war, presided aimlessly over a graft-ridden administration, conducted an incompetent and ineffectual attempt to subjugate the Southern states, and after four years was returned by the people to the obscurity that he so richly deserved.
> Donald, *Lincoln Reconsidered*.

But it is important to remember that Lincoln was in an extraordinarily difficult position: he was an *elected* leader fighting a civil war intended to bring together again the very men who were attempting to kill each other on the battlefield. If he made the wrong decisions at times, or sometimes made no decisions at all because of the complexities involved, it is not surprising!

Lincoln and the generals

Although Lincoln did not conduct the fighting, he was closely involved in the overall strategic direction of the war, and although the generals were the commanders in the field, Lincoln chose the generals.

Military historians and military experts rarely seem to agree. The heroic view of Lincoln credits him with a grasp of strategy and, in the end, with the correct direction of the war effort. The twentieth-century historian T. Harry Williams wrote: 'Lincoln stands out as a great war president, probably the greatest in our history, and a great natural strategist.' On the other hand, historians such as J.C.F. Fuller think that the victory really belonged to Grant. But even that is not the limit of the dispute, for what about all the chopping and changing of commanders which took place until Grant was created Lieutenant General? Was the President hopelessly indecisive, the victim of pressure groups in Washington? Did he interfere too much in affairs which should have been left to professional soldiers? Supporters of McClellan think so and claim that it was McClellan who was the real military genius, undermined by Lincoln's decision to recall him from the Peninsular Campaign just when he was on the verge of success.

Lincoln with Pinkerton (left), *photographed outside his tent.*

However, the chief advocate of McClellan's brilliance was McClellan himself, so perhaps we should be wary of this line of argument.

When it comes down to it, Lincoln was stuck with a real problem at the start of the war: almost all the best generals were Southerners. It took three years for the right man to emerge. That was Grant, and Lincoln chose him; to Lincoln goes the credit for ignoring the criticism of Grant's unorthodox military background and his hard drinking. Lincoln recognized Grant's most important quality: 'I cannot spare this man. He fights.'

Another 'Lincolnism'.

Hero of democracy, tyrant, or master wire-puller?

On 19 November 1863, Lincoln delivered what is perhaps the most famous speech in favour of democracy. The occasion was the burial of the dead of Gettysburg.

I.e. in 1776.

Four score and seven years ago our fathers brought forth on this continent, a new nation, conceived in Liberty, and dedicated to the proposition that all men are created equal . . . we here highly resolve that these dead shall not have died in vain – that this nation, under God, shall have a new birth of freedom – and that government of the people, by the people, for the people, shall not perish from the earth.

This reveals the way in which Lincoln believed that the aim of the war was to preserve the Union as created by the Founding Fathers.

The Gettysburg Address in Commager, *Documents of American History.*

But if the Gettysburg Address summed up the principles of constitutional freedom for which Lincoln thought he was fighting, there were plenty of people, especially in Congress, who thought that his methods of government were unconstitutional and perhaps almost despotic. He pushed the power of the executive further than it had ever been pushed before, and his chief instrument was the Presidential proclamation. At the start of the war he used proclamations to enlarge the army, to suspend Habeas Corpus, to declare the existence of a state of rebellion, and to establish a blockade of the South. Later on in the war he emancipated the slaves by means of a proclamation, and under a proclamation of December 1863 he laid down a moderate and forgiving plan of reconstruction for when the war ended.

Habeas Corpus: the right of a prisoner, held without trial, to call for a trial or else be released.

The use of proclamations depended on a rather broad interpretation of the Constitution; indeed the word 'proclamation' is not mentioned in the Article dealing with the powers of the President. It therefore took some time for Congress to ratify Lincoln's initial proclamations, and only in 1863 did the Supreme Court find them valid by a five to four majority. And in 1864

General George B. McClellan ('Little Mac') hired, fired and then electorally defeated by Lincoln.

Congress reacted against the Presidential plans for reconstruction by passing the Wade-Davis Bill, which established Congress's own far more harsh proposals. Thus:

Like all strong Presidents he enraged the Congress by sweeping and arbitrary acts that went, much of the time, beyond the Constitution – or in any case beyond the balance of Presidential and Congressional authority that is inevitably tipped in the President's favour in war time.
Alistair Cooke's America, 1973.

A Democratic senator from Delaware put it more forcefully at the time:

If I wanted to paint a despot, a man perfectly regardless of every constitutional right of the people, I would paint the hideous form of Abraham Lincoln.
Quoted in Donald, *Lincoln Reconsidered*, 1956.

But if people were thrown into jail without trial it *was* wartime, and his 'despotism' could be benevolent: he frequently used the Presidential prerogative of clemency to spare deserters from being shot. Above all, Lincoln defended himself by saying that he only ever did that which was necessary to achieve his overall aim; and it is also true that Congress and the press remained free to criticize him in outspoken terms. Ultimately he had to face the test of popular approval when it came to election time. Alistair Cooke concludes: 'Because he was not a saint, there is no obligation to see him as a tyrant or a hypocrite.'

It remains the case that Lincoln was not very popular during his Presidency; one newspaper called him 'the head ghoul at Washington'. Lincoln himself was fearful that he would not be re-elected in 1864 and that the Presidency would go to a compromise peace candidate. The question therefore remains to be asked: how did he get re-elected? The answer from the Lincoln mythology is that he *was* genuinely popular; he defeated

McClellan by half a million votes, and by a huge majority in the electoral college. Lincoln himself interpreted this as a sign of popular support for the war. But David Donald has said that a shift of just 2% of the votes cast could have resulted in Lincoln's defeat.

There is, in fact, evidence to accuse Lincoln of being merely a highly skilled political wire-puller. Nevada, despite its lack of population, was hurriedly admitted to the Union so that its three electoral votes could go to Lincoln. Thousands of soldiers were furloughed so that they could vote, and the soldier vote was in fact overwhelmingly for Lincoln; it won Pennsylvania for him by the slender margin of only 20,000 votes.

Furloughed: sent on leave.

But perhaps this is all too cynical; there is another view. By late 1864:

The war was visibly being won, and although the price remained high it was obvious that the last crisis had been passed. Sherman, Farragut, and Sheridan were winning Lincoln's election for him.

Which is to say they were winning it in part. The victory which Lincoln was to gain when the nation cast its ballots in November was fundamentally of his own making. In his conduct of the war he had made many mistakes . . . But he had gained and kept, somehow, the confidence of the average citizen of the North.
Bruce Catton, *The Civil War*, McGraw Hill Inc., 1960.

In the end, it may well be true that Lincoln ran the war like a politician, handing out patronage, playing the members of his Cabinet off against one another, manipulating the contractors and the war profiteers. But a politician is exactly what he was, and the balance of the evidence suggests that he conducted himself with humanity and without becoming power-crazed: 'He dignified the trade of politician like few men before or since.' (*Alistair Cooke's America*, 1973).

The emancipation of the slaves
On 1 January 1863 Lincoln's Proclamation of Emancipation declared that the slaves of any state still in rebellion against the Union were now free. Lincoln became 'the man who freed the slaves':

I think Abe Lincoln was next to the Lord. He done all he could for the slaves, he set 'em free.
A former slave, quoted in Donald, *Lincoln Reconsidered*.

PROCLAMATION OF EMANCIPATION.

Abraham Lincoln emancipates the slaves. (The Proclamation also contained a provision which enabled recently freed slaves to join the federal army.)

Certainly there were many people who thought that the whole point of the war was to abolish slavery:

> Since we have discerned, however, that the victory of the free North . . . will strike off the fetters of the slave, you have attracted our warm and earnest sympathy.
> Address to Lincoln by the Working Men of Manchester, England 1862; quoted in Commager, *Documents of American History*.

But Lincoln had never said that he was going to abolish slavery where it already existed; his intention was to prevent its spread:

> I have no purpose, directly or indirectly, to interfere with the institution of slavery in the states where it exists. I have no lawful right to do so, and I have no inclination to do so.
> Lincoln's First Inaugural Address, March 1861; quoted in Commager, *Documents of American History*.

For Lincoln, the *main* purpose of the war was to preserve the Federal Union. Over-enthusiatic Union officers, such as Frémont, who jumped the gun and declared slaves in captured Southern territory to be free had their orders countermanded. When in 1862 Horace Greeley wrote his 'Prayer of Twenty Million', calling on Lincoln to turn the war in to a war of emancipation, Lincoln famously replied:

An important statement, and typical of Lincoln, but the sort of statement many found it difficult to accept or understand.

> My paramount object in this struggle is to save the Union, and is not either to save or destroy slavery. If I could save the Union without freeing any slave I would do it; and if I could save it by freeing all the slaves I would do it.
> Quoted in Commager, *Documents of American History*.

The route by which Lincoln eventually came to the conclusion that it *was* necessary to free the slaves in order to save the Union is complex. One influence on him was the opinion of Liberal Republicans such as Sumner. Another was the belief that the Northern war effort could only be sustained by enlarging the purposes of the war and enlisting black support both in the North and the South. International diplomacy was also a factor; Britain was drifting towards giving recognition to the South, but would not dare to do so if the North made emancipation into a war aim.

The British government officially was neutral, although it inclined towards favouring the South; British public opinion, especially among the middle and lower classes, favoured the North.

Lincoln moved cautiously. He tried to sell Congress plans for compensated emancipation, but in July 1862 Lincoln had made up his mind. He would use the wartime powers of the President to abolish slavery in those states still in rebellion. However, under advice from Seward, Lincoln held back from issuing the Proclamation until the Union had scored a clear military victory, otherwise it would be 'our last shriek on the retreat'. It was the battle of Antietam in September 1862 which enabled Lincoln to make his policy public.

The power that he used was the Presidential proclamation, which, as we have seen, was open to debate.

What did the Proclamation of Emancipation achieve? One answer is: almost nothing.

Technically, the proclamation was almost absurd. It proclaimed freedom for all slaves in precisely those areas where the United States could not make its authority effective, and allowed slavery to continue in slave states which remained under federal control. It was a statement of intent rather than a valid statute, and it was of doubtful legality;
Catton, *The Civil War*.

A short-term interpretation. The Proclamation of Emancipation did not abolish slavery throughout the United States – it was the Thirteenth Amendment, ratified 6 December 1865, which achieved this. Furthermore, it was the Fourteenth Amendment ratified 9 July 1868, which gave the former slaves citizenship, and it took another 100 years to make this effective.

But, on the other hand:

. . . the Emancipation Proclamation changed the meaning of the war. Before the end of 1864 it had freed over a million Blacks. Territory occupied by federal troops after January I, 1863, would be free territory, and the army was now an army of liberation, however reluctant.

Blum, Morgan *et al.*, *The National Experience* Part I.

A longer-term interpretation.

In the long run, the Proclamation turned the war in to a social revolution. On 31 January 1865, Congress passed the Thirteenth Amendment, which abolished slavery throughout the United States. It was ratified on 6 December of that year, but of course Lincoln did not live to see this.

Lincoln's assassination and the problem of reconstruction

Lincoln always knew that if the Union was to be saved then the men who were his enemies in war would one day have to be welcomed as brothers. In his Second Inaugural Address (March 1865) he said:

With malice toward none; with charity for all; with firmness in the right, as God gives us to see the right, let us strive on to finish the work we are in; to bind up the nation's wounds; to care for him who shall have borne the battle, and for his widow, and his orphan . . .

Quoted in Commager, *Documents of American History*.

Another of the famous speeches which reveal the humane side of the man.

By 1865, the defeated states of Tennessee, Louisiana and Arkansas had already been reorganized under the Presidential plan for reconstruction. This allowed them to form an elected civilian government as soon as 10% of the white electorate had taken an oath of loyalty to the Constitution of the Union. This was a very lenient provision. Unfortunately, the Radical Republicans in Congress did not agree. The more principled among them thought the Southerners should be re-admitted on stricter terms; the less principled merely wanted to crush and exploit the South unmercifully. There was trouble ahead.

When the war finished, slavery was dead, secession was dead, but so was Lincoln. Five days after the surrender at Appomatox, Lincoln attended a

Lincoln's second Inauguration, 4 March 1865. 'With malice toward none; with charity for all.' Lincoln's assassin, John Wilkes Booth, was in the crowd, but could not have been very impressed by what he heard.

Lincoln had a dream in which he saw himself lying in state in the White House after being assassinated.

production of the comedy *Our American Cousin* at Ford's Theatre, Washington. There the premonition of his death that Lincoln had a few nights before came true. He was shot by an actor, John Wilkes Booth, who shouted either 'Sic semper tyrannus' ('Thus it always will be to tyrants'), or 'The South shall be free'. Lincoln died of his wounds the next morning.

Lincoln's death was received with a wave of national mourning. The grief which greeted the 15-day funeral procession around the North was real enough. However, the man who had saved the Union had left it to others to put the Union back together again, and there were unscrupulous men in Congress who regarded Lincoln's death as a great opportunity for 'radical reconstruction'. The devastated South faced a bitter future. It has often been assumed that Lincoln could have saved the South from being stripped by Northern vultures, but there is evidence that even Lincoln would have found it difficult to stop the North seeking vengeance on the South.

It is interesting to speculate how history may have viewed Lincoln if he had not attended Ford's Theatre on 14 April 1865 – Good Friday.

Not Coventry or Dresden; this is Richmond, Virginia, the Confederate capital, after its surrender in 1865.

Conclusion

From an anecdote told by Lincoln against himself.

My experience has taught me that a man who has no vices has damned few virtues.

Lincoln was an extraordinary ordinary man. His popular appeal at a national level stemmed from his humble origins and from the fact that in the end he was vindicated by success. He was the man who saved the Union, the man who freed the slaves and the man who made America safe for democracy.

On a personal level, those who knew him came to love and revere him, but he was not the stuff out of which conventional heroes are made. His physical appearance was unconventional, to say the least, and he was not orthodox in any religious sense. He was ashamed of his log-cabin background, estranged from his father, and haunted by dreams and melancholy. He possessed an almost obsessive humility which one suspects may have been employed to repress an almost equally powerful but often frustrated ambition – his frequently repeated catch phrase was, 'Why should the spirit of man be proud?' But when the Presidency loomed enticingly before him he said, 'The taste is in my mouth.'

Nevertheless, he inspired warmth and humanity, because he was himself both warm and human. His habit of telling jokes and anecdotes may have irritated the stuffed shirts of his Cabinet, but it stemmed at least in part from his ability to observe and understand human nature and human value. This carried through in to two of his great public qualities: his lack of malice and his aversion to dogmatic solutions. It also carried through into his almost religious belief in the Constitution and in republican democracy; Edwin Stanton, Lincoln's Attorney General and then Secretary of War, said of the Gettysburg Address. 'That is the voice of God speaking through the lips of Abraham Lincoln.' Lincoln himself expressed a simple but compelling view of democracy:

As I would not be a slave, so I would not be a master. This expresses my view of democracy. Whatever differs from this, to the extent of the difference, is no democracy.

Lincoln's achievements, his qualities and his human frailties certainly add up to greatness, but he was and remains a controversial figure. High office came suddenly and relatively late in a career which had been respectable but punctuated by disappointments. He may have possessed the qualities which America needed in 1860, but perhaps he was lucky to be the right man in the right place at the right time. He may have saved the Union, but equally it was the policies of his party which were helping to tear it apart (although this ignores the moral need to do something about slavery). He was hated and derided as much as he was loved and respected, during his lifetime at least. He may have been the champion of democracy, but there is a strong argument to say that he was a sectional President, about to impose sectional government on the reluctant South; no wonder the Southerners regarded him as a tyrant. He was a man of principle, but his attitudes shifted with time, his arguments had their flaws and his statements about slavery appeared to many (both slavers and anti-slavers!) disingenuous or just plain dishonest. He proclaimed the freedom of the slaves, but it took two amendments to the Constitution and a hundred years of history to make freedom or civil equality for Blacks in America anything like effective.

Perhaps the most extraordinary thing about Lincoln's reputation is that he died at the right time. At the point of his assassination he had undoubtedly been successful. If he had died at any time before 1864 he would have been regarded as a failure. If he had lived longer, he may have been able to bring his wisdom to bear on the dreadful problems of post Civil War America. But, equally, his reputation might have been seriously tarnished by failure to achieve humane reconstruction and by the dirty politics of the reconstruction era. He died leaving huge problems unsolved, but it may have been fortunate for his reputation that he did so.

The ravages of war: the last photograph of Abraham Lincoln, 10 April 1865, four days before his assassination.

Lincoln's Contemporaries

Adams, John, (1735-1826). Second President of the United States. Born in Massachusetts. A lawyer and politician, closely involved in the achievement of independence by the United States. A Federalist in the ratification disputes over the 1787 Constitution. During his presidency the passing of the Alien and Sedition Acts, together with his feud with Hamilton, contributed to the downfall of the Federalists.

Booth, John Wilkes, (1838-1865). Actor and Southern fanatic, assassin of Lincoln. Well known at Ford's theatre, Washington, and therefore able to get near the Presidential box without arousing suspicion. (Lincoln's guard had gone off for a drink.)

Brown, John, (1800-1859). Born in Connecticut, he had various occupations as a tanner, land speculator, shepherd and on the 'underground railway' helping runaway slaves. Involved in the range war in 'Bleeding Kansas', he perpetrated the massacre of five proslavers at Pottawatomie. Believing in the need for a slave insurrection, he seized the arsenal at Harper's Ferry in 1859, was captured, and conducting himself with dignity, was hanged.

Buchanan, James, (1791-1868). Born in Pennsylvania, he was a lawyer, politician and diplomat. He was Secretary of State in the cabinet of James Knox Polk (1845-9). A Democrat, he was elected fifteenth President of the United States, serving 1857-61. He regarded slavery as wrong but accepted the Lecompton Constitution for Kansas. He urged acceptance of the Dred Scott decision. He opposed secession but failed to do anything effective to prevent it during the run-up to Lincoln's inauguration. He supported the Union during the Civil War.

Calhoun, John Caldwell, (1782-1850). Born in South Carolina, he was a lawyer and politician, becoming Secretary of War (1817-1825), and serving as Vice President to John Quincy Adams and then to Andrew Jackson (1825-1829 and 1829-1833). Involved in a personal and political conflict with Jackson, he became the leading proponent of the theory of states' rights and resisted the Tariff of 1828. Nevertheless he continued to achieve greatness, for example as Secretary of State to Tyler (1844-45). He became a major apologist for slavery.

Chase, Salmon Portland, (1808-1873). Lawyer and politician, he defended fugitive slaves and became a leader of the antislavery movement. A founder of the Free Soil Party, he became a United States Senator (1849-55), and having joined the new Republican Party, he became Governor of Ohio (1855-60). Defeated by Lincoln at the Republican Party convention in 1860, he became Lincoln's Secretary of the Treasury – resigning in 1864, to be appointed Chief Justice of the United States Supreme Court.

Clay, Henry, (1777-1852). Lawyer and politician, born in Virginia, but made his career in Kentucky. Holding various public offices at national level, he was instrumental in framing the Missouri Compromise of 1820 and three times ran for President. On the second and third occasion (1832 & 1844) he was the Whig candidate, standing for tariffs and federal aid for internal improvements. Two further compromises can be added to his credit: 1833 (on tariffs) and 1850 (on slavery in the new lands gained from Mexico). He was known as "the Great Compromiser", or the "Great Pacificator".

Davis, Jefferson, (1808-1889). President of the Confederacy, he was born in Kentucky, went to West Point Military Academy and saw action at various times. Becoming a Mississippi planter, he entered politics as a Democrat and became Secretary of War (1853-57). Supporting the secession of Mississippi in 1861, he became President of the Confederacy, and was generally thought to be potentially a greater leader than Lincoln, but his autocratic methods and interference in military affairs provoked hostility.

Douglas, Stephen Arnold, (1813-1861). Born in Vermont, he made his career as a lawyer and politician in Illinois, as well as being involved in big business, such as railroad speculation. He served in the United States Congress from 1843 until his death, first as Representative then as Senator. An unashamed supporter of territorial expansion, he became chairman of the Committee on Territories, and drafted the Kansas-Nebraska Bill (1854). This incorporated the principle of popular sovereignty, which he believed would provide a fair and rapid solution to the problem of slavery in the territories, but he was wrong; instead he precipitated sectional disputes, in the midst of which his own aspirations to the Presidency was dashed. Although he is remembered for his debates with Lincoln in the contest for the Senate in 1858, he gave his complete support to Lincoln at the outbreak of Civil War.

Franklin, Benjamin, (1706-1790). Born in Massachusetts. A scientist, political thinker and statesman, he contributed greatly to the early history of the United States and the formulation of the Constitution of 1787.

Frémont, Charles John, (1813-1890). Born in Georgia, he was a soldier, explorer and politician, his travels taking him over much of the far west; his most famous action being to lay claim to California during the war with Mexico (1846). Leaving the army, he went in to politics and was the new Republican Party's first Presidential candidate, in 1856, when he came a respectable second to Buchanan.

Garrison, William Lloyd, (1805-1879). Massachusetts-born abolitionist and newspaper editor, his most famous production was the *Liberator*, which demanded complete and immediate emancipation. A founder of the American Antislavery Society (1833), he actually demanded that the *North* should secede from the federal union because the Constitution tolerated slavery. During the Civil War he supported Lincoln, once Lincoln was committed to emancipation.

Grant, Ulysses Simpson, (1822-1885). Born in Ohio, he graduated from West Point and saw action in the war with Mexico. Thereafter he tried farming, store-keeping and real estate, before finding his way again in the Union forces during the Civil War. Tough and uncompromising in battle, he distinguished himself as a commander in the western theatre and was eventually rewarded by being made Lieutenant General in supreme command. After the Civil War he entered politics and served two terms as President 1869-77, but his talents were more for soldiering than for civilian administration and his period in office was marred by public scandals.

Greeley, Horace, (1811-1872). New Hampshire-born journalist and opponent of slavery, he founded the New York *Tribune* in 1841, which became highly influential in the North. Supporting a variety of reform movements, he was a founder of the Republican Party and supporter of Lincoln in the 1860 election, but during the Civil War criticized Lincoln from a radical antislavery position.

Jackson, Andrew, (1767-1845). Born in South Carolina, he made his career as a lawyer in Tennessee, but joined the army for long enough to defeat the British at New Orleans 1815, the Seminole Indians 1818, and to invade Florida. He had a highly personal approach to politics, fighting several duels, and carrying through a feud with the Bank of the United States. President from 1829 to 1837, he had few clear principles, but characterized the shift from the patrician politics of the eighteenth century to the more open, rough and democratic politics of the nineteenth century.

Jefferson, Thomas, (1743-1826). Lawyer and polymath from Virginia. He drafted the Declaration of Independence (1776) but was minister to France during the drafting of the second great document in American history, the Constitution. Supporting a strict interpretation of the Constitution as a guarantee of liberty, he became President (1801-1809), but was more pragmatic once in office.

Lee, Robert Edward, (1807-1870). Another great Virginian, he graduated from West Point in 1829 and was a genuinely professional soldier and gentleman throughout his career. He commanded the troops which suppressed John Brown's insurrection, and in 1861 Lincoln offered him command of the federal army, but after much soul-searching Lee decided to fight for the South. He rapidly became commander of the vital Army of Northern Virginia, but perhaps surprisingly he was not made general in chief of all Confederate forces until February 1865, when it was too late. He was a highly intelligent and resourceful military leader. His home was at Arlington, across the Potomac from Washington; it is now the U.S. Military Cemetary.

McClellan, George Brinton, (1826-1885). Born in Philadelphia, he was a university student, West Point graduate, explorer, surveyor, engineer and fighting man until he left the army in 1857 to become a railroad engineer and then a railroad president. Appointed major general at the start of the Civil War, he had a controversial career in which he treated Lincoln with a lack of respect and achieved results which were good only in parts. He ran against Lincoln as Democratic candidate for the Presidency in 1864, advocating a compromise peace, but was defeated. He returned to being an engineer, and became Governor of New Jersey.

Seward, William Henry, (1801-1872). From New York State, he was a lawyer and Whig Governor (1834). Elected to the United States Senate in 1848, he strongly opposed slavery, and joined the new Republican Party. He is especially remembered for saying that there was "an irrepressible conflict" between North and South, a statement which tinged him with radicalism and contributed to his defeat by Lincoln in the contest for the Republican nomination in 1860, even though his views were generally very similar to Lincoln's own. Secretary of State to Lincoln, he continued to serve in the cabinet of Andrew Johnson, Lincoln's successor, where he tried to resist vengeful plans for reconstruction.

Sherman, William Tecumseh, (1820-1891). Born in Ohio, he graduated from West Point, fought in the war against Mexico and then went into banking, although he was unsuccessful. Joining the Northern army as a brigade commander at the start of the Civil War, he rose steadily in rank as he distinguished himself in the fighting in the western theatre, taking over from Grant at Chatenooga in 1864, marching through Georgia, to Atlanta and then Savannah. His war became one of destruction, not just of enemy troops, but of the entire economy of enemy territory; as such he has the dubious distinction of being considered the first modern general. In 1869 he took command of the United States army.

Taney, Roger Brooke, (1777-1864). Born in Maryland, he was a lawyer, and became United States Attorney General under Jackson. In 1835 he was made Chief Justice of the Supreme Court, despite Whig opposition. Although he was Chief Justice for many years, he is chiefly remembered for his contentious decision in the Dred Scott case. He also made important contributions to the interpretation of the law, for example by emphasizing community rights.

Washington, George, (1732-1799). The most celebrated Virginian of all, he fought against the French in the 1750s, became prominent in the movement for independence, and was appointed commander of the Continental army to fight the British. After the War of Independence he went into retirement, but was called back to preside over the making of the new Constitution in 1787. He was then unanimously elected President, and his great peacetime achievement was to make the new Constitution work.

Book List

This list is not intended to be exhaustive, and is confined to material generally available in Britain.

Thomas Benjamin, *The American Civil War*, 1952.
D.W. Brogan, *Abraham Lincoln*, Duckworth, 1935.
P.A. Burchell, *Westward Expansion*, (Documents), Harrap, 1974.
Bruce Catton, *The Civil War*, McGraw-Hill Inc., 1960.
Bruce Collins, *The Origins of America's Civil War*, Arnold, 1981.
Henry Steele Commager, (ed.) *Illustrated History of the American Civil War*, Orbis Publishing, 1958.
C.P. Hill, *A History of the United States*, Arnold, 3rd edition 1974.
Maldwyn A. Jones, *The Limits of Liberty*, American History 1607-1980, O.U.P., 1983.
Commager Leuchtenburg Morison, *A Concise History of the American Republic*, O.U.P., 1977.
Stephen B. Oates, *With Malice Towards None, The Life of Abraham Lincoln*, George Allen and Unwin, 1977.
Peter J. Parish, *The Amerrican Civil War*, 1975.
J.P. Pole, *Slavery, Race and Civil War in America*, (Documents), Harrap, 1974.
Robert Young and Stephen Jenkins, *The United States 1783-1877*, O.U.P. 1974
John White, *Reconstruction after the American Civil War*, Longman 1977.